# THE GAMBLING TIMES GUIDE

# BLACKJACK

## BY STANLEY ROBERTS

with EDWARD O. THORP, Ph.D., LANCE HUMBLE, Ph.D.
JULIAN BRAUN, JERRY PATTERSON,
ARNOLD SNYDER, KEN USTON,
D. HOWARD MITCHELL

A Gambling Times Book
Distributed by Carol Publishing Group

# THE GAMBLING TIMES GUIDE TO

# BLACKJACK

### BY STANLEY ROBERTS
with EDWARD O. THORP, Ph.D., LANCE HUMBLE, Ph.D.
JULIAN BRAUN, JERRY PATTERSON,
ARNOLD SNYDER, KEN USTON,
D. HOWARD MITCHELL

Carol Publishing Group Edition - 1994

Distributed by Carol Publishing Group
120 Enterprise Avenue
Secaucus, NJ 07094

**THE GAMBLING TIMES GUIDE TO BLACKJACK**
Copyright © 1984 by Gambling Times Incorporated

Manufactured in the United States of America
ISBN: 0-89746-015-4

Carol Publishing Group books are available at special discounts
for bulk purchases, sales promotions, fund raising, or
educational purposes. Special editions can also be created to
specifications. For details contact: Special Sales Department,
Carol Publishing Group, 120 Enterprise Ave., Secaucus, NJ 07094

10 9 8 7 6 5 4 3 2 1

All material presented in this book is offered as information to the reader. No
inducement to gamble is intended or implied.

## OTHER *GAMBLING TIMES* BOOKS
## AVAILABLE—CURRENT RELEASES
(See page 216 for details)

### BLACKJACK BOOKS

**The Beginner's Guide to Winning
Blackjack** by Stanley Roberts
**Gambling Times Guide to Blackjack**
by Stanley Roberts
**Winning Blackjack**
by Stanley Roberts
**Million Dollar Blackjack**
by Ken Uston

### POKER BOOKS

**According to Doyle**
by Doyle Brunson
**Caro on Gambling**
by Mike Caro
**Caro's Book of Tells**
by Mike Caro
**Free Money: How to Win in the
Cardrooms of California**
by Michael Wiesenberg
**New Poker Games**
by Mike Caro
**Poker for Women**
by Mike Caro
**The Railbird**
by Rex Jones
**Tales Out of Tulsa**
by Bobby Baldwin
**Wins, Places and Pros**
by Tex Sheahan

### CASINO GAMING BOOKS

**The GT Guide to Casino Games**
by Len Miller
**The GT Guide to Craps**
by N.B. Winkless, Jr.
**How to Win at Casino Gaming
Tournaments** by Haven Earle Haley

### GENERAL INTEREST BOOKS

**Gambling and the Law**
by I. Nelson Rose
**The GT Guide to Bingo**
by Roger Snowden
**The GT Guide to European and Asian
Games** by Syd Helprin
**The GT Guide to Systems that Win, Vols.
I and II**
**The GT Guide to Winnings Systems, Vol. II**
**GT Presents Winning Systems and
Methods, Vols. I and II**
**The GT Quiz Book**
by Mike Caro
**Golf, Gambling and Gamesmanship**
by Gary Moore
**The Mathematics of Gambling**
by Dr. Edward O. Thorp
**P$yching Out Vegas**
by Marvin Karlins, Ph.D.

*v*

**Winning by Computer**
by Dr. Donald Sullivan

## SPORTS BETTING BOOKS

**Fast Track to Thoroughbred Profits**
by Mark Cramer
**The GT Guide to Basketball Handicapping**
by Barbara Nathan
**The GT Guide to Football Handicapping**
by Bob McCune
**The GT Guide to Greyhound Racing**
by William McBride
**The GT Guide to Harness Racing**
by Igor Kusyshyn, Ph.D., Al Stanley
and Sam Dragich
**The GT Guide to Jai Alai**
by William R. Keevers
**The GT Guide to Thoroughbred Racing**
by R.G. Denis

## LIST OF TABLES AND DRAWINGS

*vii*

# TABLE OF CONTENTS

# INTRODUCTION

*The Gambling Times Guide to Blackjack* brings together in print for the very first time the men who have revolutionized the game of Blackjack:

Edward O. Thorp, Ph.D., the author of *Beat the Dealer*, who almost "broke the bank" at Las Vegas;

Julian Braun, the "computer whiz," who loves the game of Blackjack with a passion and who put together the first computerized Blackjack system;

Lance Humble, Ph.D., a university professor who teaches courses in gambling, psychometrics and motivation, is the creator of the HI-OPT I and HI-OPT II Blackjack systems;

D. Howard Mitchell, who is acknowledged by his peers as a Blackjack master, is the creator of the DHM system;

Kenneth Uston, who has probably had more media coverage than any other Blackjack expert, is single-handedly responsible for the no-barring rule in Atlantic City;

Jerry Patterson, who because of his vast knowledge of the game of Blackjack and his long association with the game, is a much sought after guest for local and national radio and television talk shows;

Arnold Snyder, who is one of the youngest Blackjack geniuses to appear on the scene, has created the irreverent comic role of Bishop Snyder whose sole purpose in life is to warn Blackjack players against placing their faith in "get-rich-quick" schemes;

Stanley Roberts, a successful entrepreneur, who has made the game of Blackjack more popular each year. He is the publisher of *Gambling Times* magazine—the only magazine of its kind in the country. He is the Blackjack guru of the 80's.

*The Gambling Times Guide to Blackjack* is clearly the most definitive book on Blackjack today—not only for the expert and advanced-level player, but for the casual player as well.

*1*

# A BRIEF HISTORY OF THE GAME

## by Stanley Roberts

The game of Blackjack is known by various other names, principal among these being: Twenty-one, Vingt-et-un (French for 21); van-john; pontoon and others. The last two are English and Australian corruptions of the French Vingt-et-un, respectively. The game is legally played in various parts of the world; some of these locations are listed below:

1. The United States: throughout the State of Nevada and Atlantic City, New Jersey.

2. Canada: The Yukon, Calgary, Alberta and various agricultural fairs.

3. Puerto Rico.

4. The Caribbean region including: Antigua, Aruba, The Bahamas, Bonaire, Curacao, The Dominican Republic: Haiti, St. Maarten, Guadeloupe and Martinique.

5. Central and South America including: Panama, Honduras, Guatemala, Argentina, Chile, Columbia, Ecuador, Surinam, Paraguay, Venezuela, and Uruguay.

6. Europe, including: England, France, Belgium, Spain, The Netherlands, Denmark, Gibraltar, Austria, Bulgaria, Hungary, Greece, Italy, Monaco, Portugal, West Germany, Malta, Romania, and Yugoslavia.

7. Africa, including: Botswana, Kenya, Lesotho, Madeira, Malagasy Republic, Ghana, Mauritius, Morocco, Nigeria, Swaziland, Togo, and Egypt.

8. The Middle East (where the situation is highly tenuous) including: Lebanon, Syria, Turkey, and United Arab Emirates.

9. Asia, including: Macao, Malaysia, The Philippines, Sri Lanka, Nepal, and South Korea.

10. Australia and New Caledonia.

Blackjack has also seen large illegal operations, many of which were sanctioned by corrupt politicians, policemen, and the public which patronized these casinos. There are a number of areas in the United States which have run wide open illegal gambling in one form or another in the not too distant past. These included:

1. Jefferson Parish, Louisiana, near New Orleans;
2. Galveston, Texas and vicinity;
3. Hot Springs, Arkansas;
4. White Sulphur Springs, West Virginia;
5. Newport and Covington, Kentucky;
6. Steubenville, Ohio;
7. New York City (both illegal and charitable games—New York is currently considering a bill on legalization);
8. The State of Washington (on Indian Reservations);
9. The State of Oregon (limited social game, generally in bars);
10. North Dakota; and
11. A lot more too numerous to mention.

According to John Scarne, the earliest records of games similar to Blackjack can be traced to writings published as early as 1570. *The American Hoyle of 1875* is one of the first references to the name of Blackjack; however, prior to the early 1900's this game was mostly a private game. The earliest time Blackjack tables appeared in casinos in this country was somewhere around 1910 and these "casinos" were the horse rooms in and around Evansville, Indiana. Although this indicates that Blackjack has been around a long time, it wasn't until recently that much was known about the game.

The subject of the history of Blackjack would make an interesting doctoral dissertation. Perhaps some student at the University of Nevada will see fit to research the subject properly and write such a book. What is important to note in the history of this game is its incredible growth in the last two decades. The growth of the game is due principally to its structure as a relatively low house percentage game and to the interest created by the publicity surrounding the fact that it actually can be beaten by a skilled player. Most of the people directly responsible for this growth are discussed later in this book.

Another point of interest is the background of the people who run the casinos. As the demand for new and larger casinos grow, more and more of the personnel who operate them will be people with immaculate credentials. The fact remains, however, that most of the experience required to run a casino came from those people who ran illegal casinos in other places. Some of these people were connected to organized crime. Some still are. By and large the casinos' gambling "act" has been cleaned up considerably. In another generation or so, casinos will be operated by people with the morality of a typical banker. At the present time, there are still a few holdovers whose actions, behavior, and characters leave something to be desired in the way of fairness and honesty.

# CHAPTER TWO

# DEBUNKING BLACKJACK MYTHOLOGY— WHAT IT IS AND ISN'T

## by Stanley Roberts

## THE MYTH

*1. Blackjack is a game of chance.*

FACT: The best proof that Blackjack is a game of skill is that casinos bar players (see Chapter 12).

*2. You can individually make a million dollars playing Blackjack.*

FACT: Those days are over; however, you can still make a good deal of money as a player, perhaps $500 a day. Persons regularly playing and winning large stakes will soon be barred and have their picture circulated among casinos. On the other hand, if you work at Blackjack for five days a week, fifty weeks a year for ten years, and average a $500 per day win...you will win $1,000,000...before taxes and expenses.

*3. Rules:*

    *a. Always insure Blackjack*

    *b. Never split tens.*

    *c. Never hit a stiff*

FACT: The Basic Strategy player should NEVER take Insurance or split tens; however, a card counter can use these options to advantage. You'll lose a great deal of money if you stand on all stiffs (see Chapter 6 for the correct strategy).

4. *Casinos are all honest.*

FACT: Cheating is rare but see Chapter 10.

5. *It doesn't matter which casino you play in.*

FACT: It sure does—the rules are different (see p. 48).

6. *The dealer wants you to lose.*

FACT: The more you win, the better the chance you will give him a toke.

7. *The dealer knows how to play (he alone knows the rules).*

FACT: If more dealers knew how to play properly, they would earn far more on the players' side of the table.

8. *Blackjack is the best casino game you can play (only if you know how).*

FACT: The average player, who doesn't know at least what is in this book, gives the house an approximate 2% advantage. The odds are better on the pass line at craps (1.414%) or at the baccarat table at 1.13%.

9. *It's okay if the dealer takes a tie. (Blackjack machines are the same as a dealer.)*

FACT: This rule gives the dealer a 9% edge which cannot be overcome by the best of players.

10. *The faster the dealer, the more the house wins.*

FACT: Whoever has the edge will win more because he plays more hands (see Chapter 10).

11. *A bad player at the table will make you a loser.*

FACT: He might upset you, but it has no effect on the cards in the long run.

12. *You can win more in Atlantic City than Las Vegas because the house's hold percentage is less in Atlantic City*

FACT: At Blackjack, the house win is related to the relative skill of the player, the number of decks in play, the percentage of the deck dealt, the speed of the dealer, the number of players at the table, the time it takes to shuffle the cards, the options available to the players, and various bonuses awarded.

The reason so many people play Blackjack is the common belief that Blackjack can be beaten—and it can. People lose at Blackjack because they have not acquired the proper system and/or have failed to make the appropriate effort to master that system to the degree that it can be played in a casino environment. Mistakes at Blackjack mean financial losses.

The percentage of hold in a casino is related as much to the characteristics of the players as it is to any other factor. For years, Atlantic City casinos have been striving to obtain hold percentages that are comparable to Las Vegas. It is unlikely this can be accomplished because the nature of Atlantic City gaming is different from Nevada's. The reality of the situation is that it is much more favorable to the casino in Atlantic City than in Vegas.

Vegas visitors have learned to budget their playing money over the length of their stay. Otherwise, they would have to go home after the first day, instead of the average four days planned for the typical trip. Therefore, they put up a smaller part of their playing bankroll. This is reflected in the figure commonly called the "drop"—the amount of playing chips purchased.

The hold is the percentage of the drop won by the house. In Atlantic City, the player is quite often there for one day only. Many cash in their entire bankroll for casino checks, rather than leaving most of it in their pockets. Since Atlantic City is still new for many, and new casinos are being opened all the time, these players may cash out and go to another casino, where they do the same. These tactics tend to increase the size of the drop, which then decreases the percent of the hold.

Atlantic City has gone through a terrible trauma over this matter, such that they eliminated the competitive advantage they had established over Las Vegas, by eliminating what they believed to be the cause of lower hold percentages: the Surrender rule. All of this has been difficult to measure because there are no sets of comparable statistics. This is due to continuous entry of new casinos, a rather large learning curve in the area of casino marketing, the marked and horrendous effect of changeable weather conditions in Atlantic City and many other characteristics which do not allow management to properly evaluate the effect of changes on the gaming environment.

# CHAPTER THREE

# THE PRINCIPLES OF THE GAME AND WHY IT CAN BE BEATEN

## by Edward O. Thorp, Ph.D.

Experience taught gamblers that games of chance could be run so that a certain "percentage" favored one side at the expense of the other side. That is, if a game was played a sufficient number of times (the "long run"), the winnings of the favored side would generally be near a certain fixed percentage of the total amount of all bets placed by the opponent. The modern gambling casino takes the side in its games that has proven in practice to be favorable. If necessary, the casino alters the rules of the game so that the casino advantage is sufficient to cover expenses and also yield a desirable rate of profit on the capital that the owners have invested.

The total amount of bets placed is called "action." For example, if I place bets of $3, $2, and $11, I have "$16 worth of action." A player who has a certain amount of capital can generally get many times that amount in action before ultimately losing his capital to the house. This contributes greatly to the excitement of gambling.

## FAILURE OF THE POPULAR GAMBLING SYSTEMS

There have been many attempts to overcome the casino advantage. A frequent approach has been to vary the amount that is bet from play to play according to various methods, some of which are simple and some of which are very complex. By way of illustration, in the Small Martingale, better known as the "doubling-up" system, the player makes an initial bet of, say, $1. If he loses, he bets $2. Then he wagers $4, $8, $16, and so on, doubling the bet each time until he wins. Then the process is repeated starting with $1 again. The bet placed following a string of losses equals the entire amount lost in the string PLUS one. A winning bet is either a $1 bet, or has been placed after a string of losses. Thus, each win results in a net profit of $1, counting from just after the last win, and the player keeps winning a dollar every few bets. However, this system has a flaw. The casino always sets a limit on the amount that may be bet. Suppose the limit is $500 and we have started by betting $1. If there is a string of nine losses ($1, $2, $4, $8, $16, $32, $64, $128, $256), the next bet called for by the "doubling-up" system is $512, and this bet is not permitted.

It seemed in practice that with this limit on bets, the casino won the same percentage of the action it normally wins, even though a player was using the doubling-up system. Thus, the doubling-up system provided no advantage whatsoever to the player. The other complicated betting schemes all seemed to have the same flaw. It was no surprise, then, when it was later proven, by the mathematical theory of probability, that for most of the standard gambling games no betting scheme can ever be devised that will have the slightest effect upon the casino's long-run advantage.

The games for which this is an established fact include those games that mathematicians call "independent trials processes." (Craps and roulette are such games.*) What this means is that

*We assume "perfect" dice and a "perfect" roulette wheel.*

each play of the game is uninfluenced by past outcomes and, in turn, has no influence on future outcomes. For example, suppose we shuffle a deck of cards and draw one card, which happens to be the four of spades. We now return this card to the deck and shuffle *thoroughly*. If we draw one card again, the chance that it will be the four of spades is no greater than and no less than the chance of its being any one of the other 51 cards. This fact has made popular the saying, "The cards have no memory."

## THE IMPORTANCE OF THE DEPENDENCE OF TRIALS IN BLACKJACK

In contrast to the previous situation, in casino Blackjack the cards do have a memory! What happens in one round of play may influence what happens both later in that round and in succeeding rounds. Blackjack, therefore, may be exempt from the mathematical arguments which rule out favorable gambling systems for independent trials games.

Suppose, for example, that the four aces appear on the first round that is dealt from a fresh, thoroughly shuffled deck. After that round is over, the cards are placed face up on the bottom of the deck and the second round is dealt from the remaining un-used cards. Now on the second round no aces can appear; there will be no Blackjacks, no soft hands, and no splitting of aces (splitting aces is highly favorable to the player). This situation of having no aces in play (which averages almost 3 percent against the player as we shall see later) continues in succceeding deals until the deck is reshuffled and the aces are brought back into play.

Some years ago one casino made a practice of removing four tens and a nine from the deck. This added 2.5% to their advantage. The Nevada Gaming Control Board brought the casino to trial. Eventually their license was revoked.

There was an ironic sidelight to the trial. The casino operators were laymen through and through and not at all theoreticians.

They knew that their short deck helped them, but they did not know how much. Thus, they had no answer for the damning assertion of an expert witness that they were putting the player not at a 2.5% disadvantage but at a 25% disadvantage!

## THE USE OF FAVORABLE SITUATIONS

Modern winning Blackjack strategies depend largely on the fact that as the composition of a deck changes during the play, the advantage in Blackjack will shift back and forth between player and casino. The advantage sometimes is 10% or more for one side or the other and on very rare occasions can reach 100%. Watch the cards that are used up on the first round of play. The fact that these cards are now missing from the deck will, in general, shift the house advantage up or down on the hands that will be dealt on the second round from the now depleted deck.

As successive rounds are dealt from the increasingly depleted deck, and the advantage shifts back and forth between player and house, we make large bets when the player has the advantage and very small bets when the house has the advantage. The result is that the player tends to win a majority of his large favorable bets, and although he tends to lose a majority of his small unfavorable bets, he tends to have a net profit.

Here is one very special example of a favorable situation that would be uncovered by someone who counted all the cards that are played in each rank, like the casekeeper does in Faro. (Note: The popular and powerful modern systems do not use such detailed and difficult counting. However, they also wouldn't detect this particular situation.) Suppose you are playing the dealer "head-on"; this means that you are the only player at the table. Suppose also that you have been keeping careful track of the cards played from each rank and you know that the unplayed cards from which the next round will be dealt consist precisely of two sevens and four eights.* How much should you bet? Answer: Place the maximum bet the casino will allow. Even borrow money if you have to, for you are certain to win if you simply stand on the two cards you will be dealt.

Here is the analysis. If you stand on your two cards, you do not bust and are temporarily safe. When the dealer picks up his hand, he finds either 7,7; 7,8; or 8,8. Since his total is below 17, he must draw. If he holds 7,7, there are no sevens left so he will draw an eight and bust. If he holds 7,8 or 8,8, he will bust if he draws either a seven or an eight—the only choices. Thus, the dealer busts and you win.

This brings us to the central problem that I had to solve in analyzing the game of Blackjack: How can a player evaluate the depleted deck in general to determine whether or not it is favorable, and if it is favorable, precisely how much so?

First I wrote a computer program to determine the correct basic (or full deck) strategy and the corresponding player advantage or disadvantage. The program was based on the methods of Baldwin, Cantey, Maisel and McDermott. It recalculated these to a higher degree of approximation. It corrected some overall inaccuracies in the basic strategy for one deck and gave the player disadvantage for one deck versus typical rules as no worse than −0.21% and probably better. Baldwin, et al, gave −0.62% but later found a calculational error which made −0.32% the number they would otherwise have given. The actual figure for their version of the basic strategy is a player *advantage* of +0.09% and the

---

*The essential thing is that there be at least three eights and at most two sevens actually available for play. For example, if the casino does not deal the last card (a frequent practice), two sevens and three eights would not work in this example. In a four-deck game one could have a similar example with as many as sixteen eights and two sevens.*

actual figure for the fully correct basic strategy is +0.13%. With variations in casino rules, or in the number of decks, these figures will change but their order relative to one another will remain the same. For instance, for four decks, subtract −0.51% from these numbers and change the basic strategy somewhat.

After recalculating the basic strategy, I developed my "Arbitrary Subsets" program to calculate the approximate best strategy and player advantage or disadvantage for any pack of cards whatsoever: 500 decks, decks with all the aces gone, decks that had fives and tens only, etc. You specify the pack and the computer does the rest.

I then solved the problem* of developing practical winning blackjack strategies by asking the IBM 704 high-speed electronic computer a series of questions. The first question was: Suppose Blackjack is played with a deck from which only the four aces are removed. What is the best possible strategy for the player to follow and what is the house (or player) advantage? In order words, the computer was to do exactly the same thing it had done in finding the basic strategy, with one difference. It had to solve the problem with a deck from which the four aces were missing.

The result was noteworthy. When playing with a deck that has four aces missing, the player is at a disadvantage of 2.42%, under best play.

It may seem that the removal of the four aces should effect matters much more than the removal of any other four cards, since aces play such a unique role in the game. They are essential for a natural and for soft hands, and they make the most favorable pair. Wherever they appear, they seem to help the player. Thus,

---

*It was solved by me to a high degree of approximation. More exact recalculations were made later by Julian Braun of the IBM Corporation using a program based on my original "Arbitrary Subsets" program.*

some players may suppose that fluctuations in the proportion of aces in the deck would have a much greater effect on things than fluctuations in the proportion of any of the other cards and that we ought simply to study aces alone. However, we will see that aces alone are not overwhelmingly important.

The computer was now asked to compute the player's advantage or disadvantage, using the best strategy, when playing with decks from which were removed in turn: four 2's, four 3's, etc. The results for these and some other special decks are listed in Table 3–1. The corresponding best strategies were computed but were omitted to save space.

Table 3–1 suggests that a shortage of cards having values 2 through 8 might give the player an advantage, while a relative excess of such cards might hurt the player. Conversely, a shortage of nines, tens, and aces ought to hurt the player, while an excess of them should help him. A variety of winning strategies may be based on counting one or more types of cards.

Most effective modern card-counting systems are based on the idea I had from Table 3–1: Give a zero or plus "point count" to cards that help the player by their removal; namely, two through eight, and a zero or minus "point count" to cards that hurt the player when they are gone; namely, aces, tens and nines. For instance, the "simple point count system" counts twos through sixes +1 as they fall, tens and aces −1, and sevens, eights and nines 0. You can see from Table 3–1 that this point count is only a rough indicator of the effects of those cards. But it has the virtue of being simple. That's the tradeoff between the various top-rated systems: power versus simplicity and ease of use. The more you have of one the less you have of the other.

(See Table 3-1 on following page)

## TABLE 3-1

### PLAYER'S ADVANTAGE OR DISADVANTAGE FOR CERTAIN SPECIAL DECKS

| Description of deck | Advantage (in percent) with best strategy |
|---|---|
| complete | 0.13 |
| Q(1)=0 | −2.42 |
| Q(2)=0 | 1.75 |
| Q(3)=0 | 2.14 |
| Q(4)=0 | 2.64 |
| Q(5)=0 | 3.58 |
| Q(6)=0 | 2.40 |
| Q(7)=0 | 2.05 |
| Q(8)=0 | 0.43 |
| Q(9)=0 | −0.41 |
| Q(10)=0 | 1.62 |
| ½ deck | 0.85 [0.93] |
| two decks | −0.25 |
| four decks | −0.41 |
| 5000 decks | −0.58 |
| Q(10)=4 | −2.14* |
| Q(10)=8 | −3.13 |
| Q(10)=12 | −1.85 |
| Q(10)=20 | 1.89 [2.22] |
| Q(10)=24 | 3.51 [4.24] |
| Q(10)=28 | 5.06* [6.10*] |
| Q(10)=32 | 6.48* [7.75*] |
| Q(10)=36 | 7.66 [9.11] |
| Q(9)=Q(10)=0 | 9.92* |
| Q(8)=Q(9)=Q(10)=0 | 19.98* |
| Q(5)=...=Q(10)=0 | 78.14 |

(See Key on following page)

Key: $Q(X)=Y$ means that a particular deck was altered by changing only the quantity $Q$ of cards that have numerical value $X$ so that there are now $Y$ such cards. For example, $Q(2)=3$ would mean that in the deck there are only three Twos instead of the usual four. "Two decks" means the cards are dealt from two ordinary 52-card decks that have been mixed together as one. The advantage with insurance is 0.12 percent greater for $Q(2)=0$ to $Q(9)=0$. The player insures only if neither of his hole cards is Ten. For $Q(10)\gtrless 20$ the advantage with insurance follows in square brackets. Always insure when $Q(10)\gtrless 20$.

*Approximate.

## EARLY WINNING PLAYERS

Most of the stories surrounding these early players are not a matter of public record or even known beyond a small circle of acquaintances. No part of the legend became known to me until sometime after I had completed the winning strategy outlined in *Beat the Dealer* and had arrived in Nevada to test it in actual play.

The first of the successful system players, a much different personality from the others in the group and in no way representative, was a colorful individual known as "Greasy John." Large and obese, he acquired his name from his habit of coming to the casino with a large bag of very greasy fried chicken. He played for as long as twenty hours at a stretch, never leaving the table. The casino supplied the drinks, and innumerable meals of varying sizes were drawn from the huge bag of chicken. It soon became apparent that "Greasy John" wanted to play alone. As crowded as the casinos are, once he became a familiar face he did not have much trouble keeping other players away. His profanity and drinking drove off all but the hardiest of women players and finally the casinos forbade all women to play at the same table with him.

Since Greasy John's hands were generally dripping with chicken fat, the cards soon became too oily to handle comfortably. Even though decks were changed frequently, the grease was sufficient to drive away the men players.

Greasy John played for long hours day after day, and in a few months he became wealthy enough to retire. He suffered a heart attack and died shortly after. We have no knowledge of the system that Greasy John used. It seems probable from surviving details that he employed end play. End play can produce astronomical gains in a short time in spite of the fact that the player's basic playing strategy is poor. Furthermore, end play is a very natural idea, easy to verify empirically, and it probably has occurred to a great many players.

To my knowledge, the first person who employed a "count" system in successful casino play was Benjamin F. ("System Smitty") Smith, a well-known figure in the Las Vegas casinos. According to Mr. Z, who has seen Smitty's voluminous notebooks, Smitty spent several years playing out 100,000 hands in an effort to determine the proper standing numbers when a ten count was employed. The system, as described to me by Mr. Z, gave a fair approximation of the totals to stand on for various values of the ratio tens/others. However, there were certain moderate errors, which resulted, at least partly, from the nature of the system.

In addition to moderate errors in standing numbers, Smitty reportedly had no detailed strategy for doubling down and pair splitting. These factors reduced the frequency of favorable bets as well as their favorableness. Also, losses increased on the small "waiting" bets. Since most of the favorable bets are in the 0% to 3% range, the win rate is greatly diminished. The alternative for the player who wants to make a big win is to overbet his capital (in terms of the theory of proportional or "fixed fraction" betting), greatly increasing the chance of ruin, and hope for the best.

Smitty probably did precisely this, for he has had many spectacular win-loss sequences. Mr. Z said he was present one night when Smitty won $108,000 at the Blackjack tables (that is a considerable sum with a $500 limit) and lost it all back by the next morning. He did not even have the price of breakfast left.

Smitty's system, which was first used in the mid-fifties, I believe, seems to have spread to a small group of players including a certain old-time gambler whom we shall call the Silver Fox, the Fox's mistress, the Mr. X (of *Beat the Dealer,* Chapter 5), Mr. Z, the "little dark-haired guy," and a young player commonly known both as "Junior" and as "Sonny."

This group of players pumped large sums of money out of the Blackjack tables within the next few years. There is no way to determine exactly how large the sums were. For what it is worth, the "grapevine" credits the Fox with $50,000 gross winnings, Mr.

Z with $56,000 gross (afterwards divided with his bankrollers), and Mr. X with $100,000 to $150,000 gross. The little dark-haired guy is supposed to have cleared $250,000. (He currently runs a casino in Las Vegas.)

In any case, the members of the group won large amounts in a short time in only a few casinos, and as a consequence the casinos, which had initially been skeptical of the possibility that the game could be beaten, finally barred each of the members of the group from play at the twenty-one tables and spread the warning.

It is obvious that casino employees are trained to remember people. Junior (also called "Sonny") told me that after he was universally barred in the casinos, he went to the make-up department of one of the Hollywood movie studios. He paid $500 for a complete disguise. On the basis of his facial structure, color, and build, they decided to disguise him as a middle-aged Chinese. The disguise even included a carapace to be fitted over his torso. He tried out his nice new outfit one evening at a casino in which there were six employees on duty who knew him. Five of them paid no attention to him. Shortly after he began to play, the sixth employee wandered over from the bar, spotted him at once, and exclaimed, "Hey, look everybody. There's Sonny all dressed up like a Chinese." Junior still keeps his beloved Chinese outfit stored away somewhere, buried under years of accumulated dust.

## HISTORY OF MATHEMATICAL ANALYSIS: THE BASIC STRATEGY

The *Basic Strategy* is what I call the best way to play Blackjack without counting cards. It depends on the number of decks the casino uses and it depends on the rules the casino follows. Once these are specified, we can in principle calculate the exact basic strategy. (The basic strategy has also been called "the optimal zero-memory strategy" and the optimal strategy versus the complete pack of cards. This last isn't quite accurate because even though the deal starts with a full pack, the player can observe the cards as they are played and can modify his strategy accordingly.)

The earliest effort to compute the basic strategy appears to have been at Los Alamos in 1954.* It was a "simulation" approach (several million hands were dealt to see what worked best). The simulation approach gets the right answer in situations where the decision is not very close (e.g., whether to double down on a total of 10 versus a dealer's 5-up) but for very close situations (such as whether to hit a total of 16 versus a dealer's 10-up), it may give an incorrect decision. Of course, the cost to the player of a strategy error is smallest in the closest situations, so simulation yields a pretty good strategy.

The next big step—and as it happened, one of the two crucial steps in the "Blackjack Revolution"—was taken by Baldwin, Cantey, Maisel and McDermott at Aberdeen Proving Ground. They used an approximate version of the exact mathematical calculation. This was better than simulation because if only the necessary calculations could be carried out, they would find the exact basic strategy and the exact player advantage or disadvantage using this best zero-memory strategy. Furthermore, Baldwin, et al, published their work (JASA, September 1956) and that's why, two years later, I happened to hear about it.

Table 3–2 lists some of the efforts at calculating the basic strategy and the player's expected win (+) or loss (−) rate. For uniformity the numbers are based on one deck and "standard" rules.

(See Table 3-2 on following page)

---

*This chapter draws upon Alan Wilson's* Casino Gambler's Guide *and Epstein's* The Theory of Gambling and Statistical Logic, *as well as my own* Beat the Dealer. *All are recommended reading.*

# TABLE 3-2
## PROGRESS IN CALCULATING THE BASIC STRATEGY
## AND CORRESPONDING PLAYER ADVANTAGE OR DISADVANTAGE

| DATE | DONE BY | METHOD | CALCULATED PLAYER EDGE | COMPUTER | NOTES · IMPACT |
|------|---------|--------|------------------------|----------|----------------|
| 1954 | Los Alamos | Simulation | −0.7% | IBM 701 | |
| 1954-57 | Wilson (General Dynamics) | Simulation and Approximate Theory | +0.05 ± 0.12% | IBM 650 | *Casino Gambler's Guide* 1965 |
| 1956 | Baldwin et al (Aberdeen) | Theory: Approximate | −0.62% −0.32% | Desk Calculator | Published—Major |
| 1956 | Epstein (Ramo-Wooldrich) | Theory: Approximate | −0.14% | Remington Rand 1103 | *Theory of Gambling and Statistical Logic,* 1967 1977 |
| 1959 | Lea (Martin) | Theory: Approximate | −0.01% | IBM 650 | |

| DATE | DONE BY | METHOD | CALCULATED PLAYER EDGE | COMPUTER | NOTES · IMPACT |
|---|---|---|---|---|---|
| 1959 | Univac (Picot) (Los Angeles) | Simulation check of Baldwin 1956 | −0.5% | Univac | |
| 1959 | Thorp (M.I.T.) | Theory: Approximate | $\geq$ = −0.21%* | IBM 704 | "Proceedings of National Academy of Science," Jan. 1961 and *Beat the Dealer* 1962, 1966, the origin of all winning blackjack card counting systems. |
| 1963-79 | Braun (IBM) (Chicago) | Successive refinements of Thorp computer program converging to exact solution | +0.13% | IBM 7090 IBM 360 | Major impact on subsequent work. |
| 1974 | Manson, Barr and Good-right (No. Carolina State University) | Exact theory except for pair splitting | −0.36%** | IBM 360-75 | Four deck basic |

# HISTORY OF MATHEMATICAL AND COMPUTER DEVELOPMENT OF WINNING CARD COUNTING STRATEGIES

During 1959 and 1960 I did the computer studies at M.I.T. that led me to the original scientific proof that there were winning Blackjack strategies. I also worked out the details of the ten-count strategy, which even now is nearly as good as the best one-parameter ("points/cards left") strategies since devised. I also worked out the general procedures for constructing and measuring the power of all "one-parameter" card-counting systems. This was indicated but not explained in the discussion of the ultimate strategy in *Beat the Dealer* (1962).

The subsequent most significant theoretical advances were, in my opinion:

1. Braun's extensive refined recalculations and extensions of my basic results;

2. Fristadt and Heath's construction of a powerful and useable two-parameter strategy;

3. Griffin's methodology for and detailed comparison of the power of various strategies;

4. The observation from many different people that aces are important in determining the bet size but do not usually affect the one-parameter strategy tables much, led to improved variations in the major strategies in which a side count of aces is kept and used for determining bet size, but not playing strategy tables; and

5. The consequent appreciation among the leading theoreticians that each point count can be measured for its power (a) as a selector of bet size, and (b) for its "efficiency" in making each strategic decision. In general a point count method will vary in power over those situations. Its overall power is due partly to how good it is as a bet size selector (60%) and due partly (40%) to how good it is at strategy decisions.

The 60–40 weight I suggest varies with circumstances. For instance, in flat betting, only the strategy table is important so the weight is 0–100. But for extreme bet size variations, the weight might be 70–30.

There have been dozens of notable theoretical contributors in addition to those I have mentioned. I regret that there is not room here to give them deserved recognition.

Besides the theoreticians, there have been several influential books on winning Blackjack. Authors include Epstein, Wilson, Revere, Roberts, Wong, Noir, Humble, and Uston. Again, there have been so many that I have surely left out several.

I wish to thank the scores of researchers who have checked and reconfirmed one or more of the winning Blackjack strategies. These independent calculations, some theoretical and some via statistical simulation, make winning Blackjack systems one of the most thoroughly scientifically established facts of the twentieth century.

(See Table 3-3 on following page)

## TABLE 3-3
## PROGRESS IN DEVELOPING WINNING CARD-COUNTING STRATEGIES

| DATE | DONE BY | SYSTEM DEVELOPED: METHOD | COMMENTS | |
|------|---------|--------------------------|----------|---|
| 1958 | Wilson | "Wilson point count" A = +4, Ten = +1, others = −1; largely "beuristic"; based on good guesses, some calculations, and successfully casino tested. | Significant preliminary work on winning strategies; generally unknown until 1965 (*Casino Gambler's Guide*); no strategy tables; point values "off"; relatively weak, but a successful winning strategy. | |
| 1959-61 | Thorp M.I.T. IBM 704 | Ten count, ultimate, and general procedure for constructing and evaluating all "one-parameter" card counting systems. Scores of special decks were theoretically analyzed. The original scientific validation of winning blackjack systems. Successfully casino tested. | The principal cause of "The Blackjack Revolution." Major impact through publication of *Fortune's Formula: The Game of Blackjack* (Dec. 1960), *A Favorable Strategy for Twenty-One*, Jan. 1961, *Beat the Dealer*, 1962, rev. 1966. The various "point counts" that were discovered were not published. Many of them were then rediscovered by many others, using my methods. | |
| 1962-79 | Thorp | Extensive assistance to, and correspondence with, principal workers in the field and numerous additional publications. | | |

| DATE | DONE BY | SYSTEM DEVELOPED: METHOD | COMMENTS |
|------|---------|--------------------------|----------|
| 1963-79 | Braun | Ditto. Also calculated strategies for Revere's books plus HI-OPT I, II. Refined Thorp program. | A major influence on the continuing development of the field. Tested comparative power of various counting methods. |
| 1963 | Dubner | HI-LO 2-6 = +1, 7-9 = 0, ten, Ace = -1. Strategy tables had many inaccuracies. However, this led to point count and complete point count (*Beat the Dealer*, 1966) and HI-OPT I, II (Braun, 1970). | In 1960 Shannon and Thorp discussed this and similar variants. Thorp had finished all the computer runs needed to construct the strategy but put it aside. |
| 1967 | Griffin | Extensive testing of comparative power of various methods. In that case, a developer of all systems. | Griffin has analyzed many subtle aspects of the game and has uncovered unsuspected structural peculiarities. |
| 1969-70 | Fristadt, Heath | The first "two parametid" system: count 2-5, 6-9, 7's and "Aces on side." | Somewhat more powerful, but considerably more difficult than any one parameter system. |

## ADVANCES IN TECHNIQUE

The theoretical advances since 1962 have been accompanied by advances in technique. In 1962, *Beat the Dealer,* in the section entitled "The Enormous Advantage of Teaming Up With Other Players," I explained some of the advantages of "team play." Ken Uston ("The Big Player") and company, with the added improvement of the roving "Big Player," has made dramatic and profitable use of team play.

Again in 1962, on page 191 of *Beat the Dealer,* I said, "It is possible to build miniature low-cost readily concealed mechanical or electronic devices on which the player can count the cards..." A number of such devices have subsequently been marketed.

In 1966 (*Beat the Dealer,* rev., pp.178-179), I proposed perfect play via a radio link to a high-speed computer. Since then, with the electronic calculator/computer revolution in speed and miniaturization, it has become possible to build a tiny concealed computer which the player wears and which tells him to good approximation the bet size and decisions for playing his hand. Successful devices of this kind have reportedly been made and used.

Other techniques have been developed to locate cards. One, called "localization," keeps track of ten-ace-rich regions of the used cards, if they are not dispersed in the shuffle. Then, without counting, the player can detect "good hands coming." Another, which I published in a paper on non-random shuffling, explains how to predict the appearance of aces shortly before they are dealt (one-deck game only). A third, old technique, known as the "tell," and used by me since 1961, is now quite well known. When the dealer gets an ace or ten-up, he checks to see if he has Blackjack. Watch how far he bends the cards when he checks his hole card. With some dealers, this will tell you what he has. This leads to a clever method credited to Wong called "the warp fold." It's based on the idea that aces and tens get beaten faster on the average than other cards. As the deck ages, they become more and more identifiable.

## BLACKJACK SYSTEMS: SIMPLICITY vs. ACCURACY

The prospective winning Blackjack player faces a flood of systems and advice. How can he find his way? Before he knows enough to critically evaluate for himself, the beginner should limit himself to the advice of "recognized experts." (Even here there may be pitfalls. For instance, one well publicized casino-employed clown passes himself off as "the greatest" and claims the scientific card-counting systems are swindles. What this casino employee doesn't tell you is that while he tries to persuade you from taking up card counting, the casinos are making headlines by banning successful counters.)

My recommendation is to start with a simple strategy. Play it at home under casino rules and conditions. If and when you win consistently, go to the casino and play for small stakes only. If you again are able to win consistently, only then consider increasing your bet size and learning a more powerful strategy.

Here is one outline of the path from beginner to expert.

1. Learn a Basic Strategy (one, two or four decks, depending on where you plan to play; the three strategies are so close that any one can be used for all three without serious loss).

2. Learn a simple point count which can be "upgraded" to add a strategy table for playing hands and to add a side count of aces. One such is 2,3,4,5,6 = +1; 7,8,9 = 0; ten = −1; ace = −1. Use this for bet size. Use the Basic Strategy for playing hands.

3. Convert the simple point count to a "true" count by dividing by the number of decks left to be played. Use this for bet size and use Basic Strategy for playing hands. More accurate, but also more difficult and probably not worth the extra effort: divide by the exact number of cards left. The "index" for "The Complete

Point Count" *Beat the Dealer,* revised) is this figure times 100. Therefore, twice the index is approximately points/decks left and therefore this chapter can be converted to that easier method by doubling all the given index values for betting and strategy.

4. Add the strategy tables (*Beat the Dealer* revised, Chapter 7), replacing the Basic Strategy in steps: (a) hard drawing and standing, (b) hard doubling, (c) soft drawing and standing, (d) pair splitting, and (e) soft doubling if applicable. (Remember to double the index in all tables if you use true count = points/decks left.)

5. Add a side count of aces: 3,4,5,6 = +1; 2,7,8,9 = 0; tens = −1, aces separate. Use ace side count to bet more on ace rich packs (four aces per deck left), less on ace poor packs (less than four aces per deck left). Use points/decks left (or points/cards left) for true count. Use true count and same strategy tables as in Step 4. That's because the strategy tables are approximately the same. Note: Somewhat more exact strategy tables and details are sold such as the HI-OPT I system. But, for less than $3 you can play nearly as well.

Each step above should be learned and successfully played at home under casino conditions, then successfully played for *small stakes* at the casino before either upping the stakes or advancing to the next step.

The beauty of this outline is that everything you learn is used from then on, and at each level there is no known Blackjack system which is both significantly simpler or significantly more powerful.

This example illustrates how I think you should plan CAUTIOUSLY to advance your skill in small steps rather than plunging all at once into a complex high-level system. Remember, a GOOD system has an expected net win of roughly two big bets per hour. That means two blunders per hour on crucial hands can lose you your edge.

## WHY THE HOUSE WILL NOT LOSE

By now it is clear that it requires planning, concentration and practice to become a skilled Blackjack player. These obstacles block most ordinary Blackjack players from becoming winning card counters. (Remember, the Basic Strategy is easy enough for nearly everyone and puts you even, or almost even, with the house.) Other factors are discipline, desire, self-confidence, and a belief that the game can be beaten. Also, many people who gamble do so to lose, suffer or punish themselves. Winning is psychologically unacceptable to them.

Even so, there are hundreds of expert count players and thousands of good ones. Why aren't the casinos being cleaned out? For each million dollars the good players win, the average players may return a hundred million dollars to the casinos. The good players win but the casinos win so much more from the average players that it "doesn't matter."

The publicity to the effect that the game can be beaten has increased Nevada Blackjack interest and Blackjack revenues—both of which have grown much faster than either revenues from all table games (including craps, roulette, baccarat) or total statewide gaming revenues.

There also is a steady "graduation" of Blackjack experts. The Salmon* used his winnings to buy a fleet of taxicabs. Roberts is now a publisher/entrepreneur/Blackjack teacher. Many are selling systems, not because they can't play but because the glamour and sparkle has worn off and they're sick of the sleazy casino grind. I've gone on to the greater, more challenging and far more lucrative casino called Wall Street. The "little dark-haired guy"

---

*\*see* Beat the Dealer, *revised.*

runs a casino now. Mr. Y is a multi-millionaire jet setter who marries tennis champions and copper heiresses. Some players don't want to spend so much of their lives in a casino environment. The best counter in the world at the time (two decks, all ten ranks) when asked for a brief description of Las Vegas, said "Disneyland for the Mafia." Some players find that besides their talents that make them Blackjack greats, they can win in real estate, science, the stock market, law and even movie making.

Jerome Skolnick, in *House of Cards,* nicely summarizes why the house will not lose.

The gaming authorities find themselves in a characteristic dilemma over the issue of "counting." Privately, they regret the avariciousness and short-sightedness of the industry, especially when players are roughed up by security guards. Still, the authorities recognize that when a major newspaper like the *New York Times* publishes a lead Sunday magazine article on the problems of "counters," the article serves as an advertisement for gaming, whether intended or not. From Thorp through Ken Uston—who teaches counting methods—the message is two-pronged: one is, Nevada casinos violate the "rights" of counters; the other is, if you learn to count, you can win at Blackjack.

But few players enjoy either the ability or the bankroll to turn the percentages around, and to exploit the advantage of the edge. Casinos win because of volume. An individual player can lose in an evening even with an edge. Thus, in the long run, so-called "negative" publicity benefits the casinos by drawing players to Nevada who are not skilled counters, but think they are. The presence of such players provides the clubs with a population that makes the edge prevail.

## GROWTH IN BLACKJACK REVENUE IN NEVADA

The graph (Table 3-4) compares gross gaming revenue, including the portion of the revenue from all table games, and the part of that from Blackjack. Gross gaming revenue is defined in law as the total of all sums received as winnings less only the total of all sums paid out as losses (operating expenses are not gaming losses). All table games include: craps, roulette, '21,' keno, bingo, faro, chuck-a-luck, wheel of fortune, baccarat.

Game and table revenue probably mean "games" (twenty-one, craps, roulette, baccarat, and other games) plus "other gaming" (keno, poker, bingo and miscellaneous).

Table 3-4 (graph) and Table 3-5 (chart) compare "21" games and "all table games." We see from the graph and the table that Blackjack revenues rose at a much more rapid rate than game and table revenues, especially in the 1967-72 period. Also, Blackjack revenues (as shown in the table) have produced an increasing share of such revenue.

See following pages for Table 3-4 (graph) and Table 3-5 (chart).

# TABLE 3-4

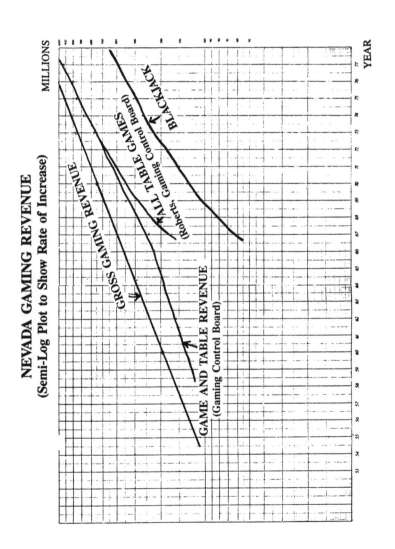

NEVADA GAMING REVENUE
(Semi-Log Plot to Show Rate of Increase)

## TABLE 3-5

### GROWTH OF "21" COMPARED TO GROWTH OF ALL TABLE GAMES*

| FY | "21" GAMES REVENUE (000) | ALL TABLE GAMES* REVENUE (000) | "21" AS PCT. OF ALL GAME REVENUE |
|---|---|---|---|
| 1967 | $ 59,051 | $169,742 | 34.8 |
| 1968 | $ 82,867 | $234,808 | 35.3 |
| 1969 | $107,418 | $299,896 | 35.8 |
| 1970 | $132,195 | $357,211 | 37.0 |
| 1971 | $149,205 | $402,284 | 37.1 |
| 1972 | $174,378 | $453,200 | 38.5 |
| 1973 | $213,936 | $544,576 | 39.3 |
| 1974 | $267,114 | $657,078 | 40.3 |
| 1975 | $308,916 | $747,471 | 40.9 |
| 1976 | $335,535 | $792,209 | 42.4 |
| 1977 | $395,057 | $886,615 | 44.6 |

*All Table Games include: craps, roulette, "21," keno, bingo, faro, chuck-a-luck, wheel of fortune, baccarat.

It is very plausible from the figures that Blackjack revenues increased even more drastically in the period prior to 1967. Unfortunately, separate Blackjack figures are not available before 1967. I speculate that the publicity from *Beat the Dealer* and subsequent books and winning players educated and attracted large numbers of players to the game. There appears to have been a major shift of less revenues to Blackjack. How much of this is new casino revenue which would not otherwise have been gained, and how much is due to a transfer of revenue from other games is not clear to me from the data.

What is clear is that (1) there is no evidence from the graph that count players are hurting gross gaming revenue, and (2) Blackjack revenue has grown rapidly compared with other revenues listed, so count playing and publicity about beating the game have accompanied a boom in Blackjack revenues.

The casino efforts to bar count players may therefore lead to a gain or even a loss in revenues, and appear to me to be foolish. If I were in charge, I'd approach it differently:

1. I would introduce certain subtle but effective rule changes which would greatly reduce the problem without serious side effects,

2. I'd "join" the count players to the extent of sponsoring tournaments, and I'd use them as "advisors," as well as to teach Blackjack and other gaming classes (which would pay for themselves through charges) to customers,

3. I'd further capitalize on the Blackjack boom by consumer testing variants (e.g., a rotating dealer, among the players, where the house collects a fee as in poker; duplicate Blackjack and duplicate Blackjack tournaments).

# CHAPTER FOUR

# THE RULES OF CASINO BLACKJACK
## PART I: THE BASIC RULES

### by STANLEY ROBERTS

The object of the game of Blackjack is to BEAT THE DEALER by obtaining a total of points equal to or less than twenty-one, so that the player's card total is higher than the dealer's. The player can also have any total less than twenty-one if the dealer *busts* his hand by getting a total of twenty-two or more. The emphasis is *not* on getting the closest one can to twenty-one without going over twenty-one or *bust*—the object is to BEAT THE DEALER.

The game of Blackjack has a dealer and generally from one to seven players. From the player's point of view, the fewer players the better.

Blackjack is played with one, two, four, five, six, or eight 52-card decks. The multiple-deck games are becoming more popular from the casino's point of view, but are discouraging many players who prefer to play with a single deck.

## THE SHUFFLE AND CUT

The cards are shuffled thoroughly by the dealer and offered to one of the players to cut. The cut is performed by hand placing one portion of the deck alongside the other, or by insertion of a joker or blank card into the deck at that place where it is to be cut. In the single-deck game, when the cards are hand-cut, it is normal to *burn* (turn face up on the bottom) the top card. This is usually done in such a manner that the players cannot see what the card is. In the multiple-deck games, where a *shoe* (dealing box) is used, it is normal practice to place the cut-card about three-fourths of the way back in the pack. This signals the dealer at which point he is to begin a new shuffle. Some casinos insert the card as little as one-half of the way back. The closer to the end of the pack the cut-card is placed, the more favorable the game is to the player.

## BETTING

All players place their bets (usually with the casino's chips) in front of them, usually into a small circle or rectangle directly in front of each player, before any cards are dealt. A player may play more than one hand, but must usually place twice the minimum wager if playing two hands, and three times the minimum wager if playing three hands. The minimum bet varies from fifty cents to $100, although it is typically two to three dollars in most large casinos. The maximum bet varies from $25 to $3,000. Some casinos have been known to raise their maximum (particularly when they think they have a sucker). Some smaller casinos which have only one or two tables may have lower maximums down to $10. The ability to vary the size of the bet is the principal advantage a player enjoys over the casino. Except on a player's Blackjack, or on an insurance bet, the settlement of the wager is made on an even money basis: one dollar paid for one dollar bet.

## THE DEAL

The dealer, starting at his left, deals each player a card in turn, then one to him. Each player and the dealer then are given a second card. One of the dealer's cards (usually his first one) is dealt face up; the other, face down. The players' cards are either dealt all face up, or all face down. In some casinos, the dealer may not take his second (face-down) card until all the players have finished drawing their cards.

## THE VALUE OF THE CARDS

All the picture cards (King, Queen, Jack) count as ten points. All the other cards count as their face value, except the ace which—at the player's option—can count either as one point or eleven. When a hand contains an ace that can be counted as *eleven* instead of *one,* without the total exceeding twenty-one, that hand is referred to as a *soft hand.* Any other kind of hand is referred to as a *hard hand.* For example, a hand containing 10,8 would be a *hard eighteen.* A hand containing ace,7 and 10 is also a *hard eighteen,* since this hand cannot count the ace as eleven because the total points would be over twenty-one (the total would be twenty-eight). A hand that contains an ace and 7 could be either a *soft eighteen* or a *hard eight.*

## BLACKJACK

When the player or the dealer is dealt an ace and a ten-value card (King, Queen, Jack, or 10) as his first two cards, he is considered to have a *natural,* or automatic winner. When the player receives this kind of hand, he turns over his cards immediately. He is paid when his turn comes, generally at the rate of 3-to-2, or 1-1/2 times his original wager. When the dealer has Blackjack, he immediately collects all wagers, except in the case where a player also has Blackjack, which is considered a standoff or *push.*

## THE DRAW

Starting with the player on the dealer's left and following around to the next player, and finally to the dealer, each player may elect to *stand* (draw no additional cards), *hit, split, double down,* or *surrender* his hand in accordance with the House Rules. If the player *stands* (also called *staying pat* or *sticking*), he usually signals this move by placing his cards under his wager. In the case of the face-up games, he indicates *standing* by placing his palm down on or above the table. A player may continue to draw cards to his hand, one at a time, by calling for a *hit* (an additional card), until that player chooses to *stand,* or he *busts* (gets a total of cards greater than twenty-one). A *hit* is generally signalled by the player scratching his cards toward himself or, in a face-up game, by beckoning with his finger. When he *busts,* he automatically loses his bet on that hand. The player is required to turn his cards face up immediately, and the dealer collects his bet and cards at that time. This is the ONLY advantage the dealer has over a good player. Should the dealer also *bust* (also referred to as *going broke* or *breaking*), he has already collected the wagers of the players who have done the same. All of the cards played are placed face up on the bottom of the deck in a rack to the dealer's right or to the rear of the cards in the shoe after the settlement.

## THE DEALER'S STRATEGY

The dealer does no thinking about the manner in which his hand is played. If his initial hand totals seventeen, eighteen, nineteen, or twenty, he must stand after the players have played their hands. He pays all hands that are greater, collects from all hands that are lower, and ties (pushes) with all equal hands. If the dealer has a two card twenty-one, a *natural,* he collects from all players not having the same. If the dealer has a total of sixteen or less, he must continue to hit his hand until it totals at least seventeen or busts. He cannot hit a hand that totals seventeen or more. Some casinos also rule that the dealer must hit a *soft* seventeen. This rule gives the house a slightly greater edge. Aside from this variation, there is little difference in the dealer's strategy. Should you ever come across a game where the dealer wins all ties, forget it. You are giving the house a significant 9% advantage!

## PLAYER'S OPTIONS

In addition to receiving additional cards, the player has several options at his discretion which are not available to the dealer. These options are granted in different degrees by various casinos or may not be permitted at all.

The first option is called a *Pair Split.* If the player has two cards of the same denomination (that is two aces, deuces, nines, etc.), he may choose to turn them face up and put up an amount of money equal to his original bet, playing each card as a separate new hand. Although 10's may also be split, some casinos require that they be of the same order (that is two Jacks, rather than a Queen and a King).* Most casinos consider all ten value cards to be pairs. Except for aces, each new hand is played out separately before cards are drawn on the second hand. Split aces are dealt only one card each, face down, in most casinos. In the case of the other pair splits, should an additional card of the same denomination as the split card come up, in effect making another pair, that card may be split again as a third hand, and so on. Some casinos also have rules as to the number of split hands, such as four hands only, or two hands only.

The second option is referred to as *Doubling Down.* When a player feels he has a good hand with his first two cards, and that it will become a very good hand with one additional card, he may turn his two cards face up, double his bet, and receive one

---

*Two ten-value cards of different denominations are sometimes called a "mixed marriage," a term used in Pinochle.*

and only one additional card, usually dealt face down. Some casinos only permit this with a two-card total of ten or eleven. Others will with nine, ten or eleven, while many permit this on any two-card hand. When one of the two cards held is an ace, this is referred to as *Soft Doubling,* since the player has a soft hand initially.

The third option is referred to as *Insurance.* When the dealer's face-up card is an ace, some casinos offer the player a side bet as to whether or not the dealer has a ten-value card in the hole (making his hand a natural and an automatic winner). The dealer must offer *insurance* BEFORE he looks at his hold card (to prevent him from giving it away by facial expression). *Insurance* is the most misunderstood option in the game of Blackjack. Most players think that they are insuring a good hand they may have when, in fact, all they are betting on is whether or not the dealer's hole card is a ten-value card. *Insurance* is paid at the rate of *two units for each one unit bet.* The player is allowed to bet only one-half of his original bet. In this case, if the dealer has a 10 in the hole (or Blackjack), the player loses his original bet and wins the insurance side bet, thereby retaining his original bet. If the dealer does not have a 10 in the hole, the player loses the insurance bet and must play his hand as he would normally.

The last option available to the player is referred to as *Surrender.* It originated in the Far East, and is gaining popularity with the Nevada casinos, although most do not offer this option at present. Simply stated, when the player looks at his hand and the dealer's face-up card, then decides that he has the worst of it, he may throw in his hand before drawing any other cards, surrendering half of his original bet. In New Jersey, the player may surrender his hand before the dealer checks his hole card. Thus, he could conceivably surrender when the dealer has a Blackjack (before the dealer looks, of course). This rule is called *Early Surrender.**

---

*\*Surrender was removed as an option in Atlantic City in May of 1981. It may be reinstated as you read this.*

# PART II: VARIATIONS IN THE GAME

# by LANCE HUMBLE

Blackjack is dealt with many rules and procedural variations in different casinos throughout the world. The effects of common variations on your chances are summarized in Table 4-1 at the end of this chapter.

In Nevada there are still single-deck games as well as two-deck, four-deck, five-deck and six-deck games. Atlantic City deals six- and eight-deck games. Four-deck games are the rule in every country outside of the United States except France where six-deck games are dealt. A single-deck game, if honest, is most favorable to the player. In general, the more decks, the tougher the game is to beat.

## THE CUT CARD

The position of the *cut card* also has an effect on your advantage if you use a *count* strategy. Some casinos cut off only half a deck in a four-deck game (12-1/2%) while others cut off as much as half a deck in a single-deck game (50%) or as many as two decks in a four-deck game (50%). Currently, most casinos cut off about 33-1/3% of the deck(s). This enables a good counter to win in these casinos. It is extremely difficult to obtain a significant advantage in a game where only 50% of the cards are dealt out.

## THE HOLE CARD

In casinos outside Nevada the dealer does not take (or look at) his *hole* card until the players have finished playing. In such cases the player using Basic Strategy faces an extra .13% disadvantage with one exception: If the dealer does not take the player's extra bets, made by splitting pairs or doubling down, then the .13% disadvantage is wiped out. If the exception is not in effect then the player should never split or double against a dealer's ten or ace.

## SOFT SEVENTEEN

In Reno, Lake Tahoe and in Downtown Las Vegas the dealer hits a *Soft Seventeen*—a hand in which the ace initially counts as "11" and not as "1." This rule is bad for the player as it gives the house an extra +.20%.

## CASINOS IN THE UNITED STATES

On the Las Vegas Strip many casinos allow surrender (+.06%) and doubling after splitting (+.10%). Doubling on any first two cards is allowed in ALL Las Vegas Strip and Downtown casinos.

The Downtown Las Vegas rules are slightly less favorable than the Strip rules because the dealer hits a soft seventeen (−.20%).

Reno and Lake Tahoe have still less favorable rules because the dealer hits a soft seventeen (−.20%) and the player is limited to doubling down only on hands of 9, 10, or 11. No soft doubling is allowed (−.14%).

## CASINOS OUTSIDE THE UNITED STATES

Rules in foreign casinos are almost without exception worse than U.S. casino rules.

In Puerto Rico, at one time, a player was allowed to double only with a hand of 11 (−.84%). This was a tremendous disadvantage considering the fact that four decks are dealt (−.54% on top of −.84% = −1.38%).

Puerto Rico now has rules similar to Atlantic City. This came about due to the competition between these two resort destinations.

In the Bahamas there is no resplitting of pairs (−.05%) and no soft doubling (−.14%).

In Aruba the dealer does not take a hole card and there is no soft doubling.

In Haiti the dealer hits a soft seventeen and no resplitting of pairs is allowed.

In Great Britain there is no soft doubling and no splitting of fours, fives, or tens.

## BARRING OF PLAYERS

Most casinos in the world have barred players even though barring may be illegal in those countries or states. Some casinos bar anyone who wins a lot of money in a short time even if they win it by luck. Some casinos are extremely paranoid about allowing players to win. Other casinos only bar players who jump their bets AND win large amounts of money (they don't care how great your bet range is if you are a loser!).

Some casinos *bar* winning players by dealing to them only one hand then they shuffle up and start over. Other casinos who deal four or more decks will cut off two or more of the decks on winning players, thus effectively barring him from winning if not from playing.

In Panama counters have been arrested for *cheating*. Some Las Vegas casino operators categorize counting as *intellectual cheating*.

I do not agree. Players should not be prevented from using their God-given ability and hard-learned skills to play Blackjack well. The American Civil Liberties Union takes the same stand as I do. Unfortunately, the State Gaming Commissions of Nevada and New Jersey have taken the side of the casinos.

If the casinos persist in barring winning players, they will kill the game. Even now many players who are members of the International Blackjack Club are turning away from Blackjack and becoming involved with sports and horse wagering. They are turning away from Blackjack because of the casinos' policies to bar players, to introduce six- and eight-deck games and to deal less than 75% of the cards. Greed on the part of the casinos will kill Blackjack as their most lucrative source of income by 1990. If the casinos were wise and looked to the future they would liberalize the rules and stop barring players. Then they would make more money from Blackjack than they ever dreamed possible. Why? Because every gambler in the world would turn to Blackjack with the knowledge that it is a game of skill which can be beaten.

## RULES VARIATIONS PERCENTAGES—
## HOW THEY AFFECT YOUR CHANCES

The Percentage Table below presents the effects of various rules on a player's advantage. The variations assume you are playing basic strategy. Using basic strategy in a single-deck game with Las Vegas Strip rules (no doubling after pair splitting and no surrender) your advantage is exactly 0.00 (an even game).

The best rule for the player is *Early Surrender*—the option to give up half of your bet BEFORE the dealer looks at his hole card. This is worth +.62% to the player using basic strategy. This rule gives the player a permanent advantage on the house even in a six-deck game.

The most damaging rule for a player is the restriction of doubling to eleven only. This gives the casino an extra .84% advantage.

**TABLE 4-1**

| RULES VARIATIONS | WITH BASIC STRATEGY |
|---|---|
| | % |
| Drawing any number of cards to split aces | +0.14 |
| Doubling allowed on any 3 cards | +0.19 |
| Doubling allowed on any number of cards | +0.20 |
| Surrender | +0.06 |
| Early Surrender | +0.62 |
| Doubling allowed after splitting | +0.10 |
| | |
| No resplitting of pairs | −0.05 |
| No soft doubling | −0.14 |
| No doubling on 9 | −0.14 |
| No doubling on 10 | −0.56 |
| Four or more decks | −0.54 |
| Two decks | −0.38 |
| Dealer hits soft 17 | −0.20 |
| No hole card | −0.13 |
| Dealer wins ties | −9.00 |

# CHAPTER FIVE

# BRIEF BIOGRAPHIES OF THE EXPERTS

## EDWARD O. THORP, Ph.D.

Edward O. Thorp, Professor of Mathematics, University of California at Irvine, is the author of the best-seller *Beat the Dealer: A Winning Strategy for the Game of Twenty-One*, the newly published, *The Mathematics of Gambling*, and is co-author of *Beat the Market*, an introduction to the techniques of convertible hedging.

*Beat the Dealer* was the forerunner of all the Blackjack systems that have proliferated since 1962. Edward O. Thorp is the Albert Einstein of gaming theory; he holds a special niche in gaming history.

Dr. Thorp has also written *Elementary Probability* and numerous mathematical papers on probability, game theory, and functional analysis. Presently, he is applying his stock market theories by acting as portfolio manager for several institutions. He is the President of Oakley, Sutton Management Company and Chairman of the Board of Oakley, Sutton Securities Corporation.

Before joining the Irvine faculty, Dr. Thorp taught at the University of California, Los Angeles; the Massachusetts Institute of Technology; and New Mexico State University. He received his Ph.D. in mathematics at UCLA and is a member of the American Mathematical Society.

Dr. Thorp lives with his family in Southern California.

## LANCE HUMBLE, Ph.D.

Lance Humble, a pseudonym for Igor Kusyshyn, Ph.D., is a Professor of Psychology at the University of Toronto and a research psychologist who teaches courses in gambling, psychometrics and motivation. He has authored four books on gambling including *The World's Greatest Blackjack Book* (with Dr. Carl Cooper), *Harness Racing Gold, The Gambling Times Guide to Harness Racing* (with Al Stanley and Sam Dragich), and *Blackjack Gold*.

Dr. Humble has also developed, with the aid of a computer, winning systems for blackjack, hockey, football and racing. His students have won millions of dollars with his systems. Each of his systems carries a guarantee to show a profit on any statistically fair sample of events.

Lance Humble and his students have conducted and published research studies on the psychology of professional and social gamblers. They have developed a new theory of human motivation on the basis of their research findings.

Humble is a member of many professional associations including the New York Academy of Sciences, the British Society for the Study of Gambling, the U. S. and Canadian Trotting Associations, the American Psychological Association, and the Canadian Psychological Association. He is listed in the Directory of American Men and Women of Science. Humble received his B.A. in Psychology and Sociology with honors from McMaster University in 1963. He received his M.A. and Ph.D in Psychometrics from the University of Western Ontario in 1964 and 1967, respectively.

## JULIAN H. BRAUN

Julian H. Braun, an instructor at IBM Advanced Education Center in Chicago, was the first person to compute Blackjack probabilities exactly and the first to compute an exact Basic Strategy.

Braun's data have been the basis for many Blackjack systems

including the revised version of Dr. Edward O. Thorp's ten-count strategy. The complete point-count strategy presented by Dr. Thorp in his book, *Beat the Dealer,* was based principally on calculations performed by Braun at IBM.

Braun who authored, *The Development and Analysis of Winning Strategies for the Casino Game of Blackjack,* published in 1974, has degrees in both mathematics and physics. His undergraduate work was completed at the Illinois Institute of Technology and his graduate work at San Diego State College.

Braun's latest book, *How to Play Winning Blackjack,* was published in 1980 by Data House Publishing, Co., Inc., Chicago.

Julian Braun, who was born in Chicago, still makes his home there.

## STANLEY ROBERTS

Stanley Roberts, a pseudonym for Stanley Robert Sludikoff, is a successful entrepreneur who is involved in several businesses, the most satisfying of which is his publishing enterprise, Gambling Times Incorporated.

Roberts, who is the author of *Winning Blackjack, How to Win at Weekend Blackjack,* and *The Beginner's Guide to Winning Blackjack,* is considered the "Blackjack Guru of the '80's."

Basing his strategy on Edward O. Thorp's, *Beat the Dealer,* Roberts, because he shuns the complex, looked for an easier way to win at Blackjack. He discovered it and played—the money began rolling in, but Roberts found that when he could win nearly all the time, the game wasn't as exciting anymore.

He decided then to write *Winning Blackjack,* which delineates his winning system, and shortly thereafter, to start his publishing empire, retiring from three concurrent careers as an architect, city planner, and real estate broker.

Today, Roberts publishes the very successful *Gambling Times* magazine, which has a readership of 250,000. He also publishes gambling books by other authors many of which have become best-sellers. He generously shares his time and expertise with those who request it.

Roberts resides in Southern California with his wife and three daughters.

## JERRY L. PATTERSON

Jerry L. Patterson, who holds a Bachelor of Science Degree in Mathematics from Willamette University and a Master of Science in Business Administration from George Washington University, is a professional Blackjack player. Before becoming a professional player, Patterson was phenomenally successful in the computer science field. When the casinos in Atlantic City opened 1978, he sold his computer company and changed careers.

Patterson, author of *Blackjack: A Winner's Handbook, Blackjack's Winning Formula,* and *Casino: Winning Techniques for Craps, Roulette, Blackjack and Baccarat,* is a syndicated Casino Gaming Columnist who is in demand for radio and television appearances across the country.

Patterson is the founder of ten Blackjack Clinics in the United States and Canada. His Blackjack Newsletter is published quarterly and sent to subscribers all over the world. More information about the Blackjack Clinics can be obtained by writing Patterson at P.O. Box 796, Cherry Hill, N.J., or calling him at (609)772-0350.

Jerry Patterson resides in New Jersey with his wife and three children.

## ARNOLD SNYDER

Arnold Snyder is the 36-year-old author of three books on casino Blackjack: *The Blackjack Formula,* published in 1980, *Blackjack for Profit,* published in 1981, *Blackbelt in Blackjack,* published in 1983.

Snyder, a sought after radio and television personality, has edited and published a quarterly journal, *Blackjack Forum,* since 1981. He is also the author of numerous articles on Blackjack.

Snyder, founder of the First Church of Blackjack, has appeared

*54*

many times on talk shows as Bishop Snyder. In this irreverent comic role, he warns Blackjack players against placing their faith in the "get-rich-quick" schemes which pervades so much of the promotion and advertising for gambling systems.

Arnold Snyder is a pseudonym. He supplies no data on his actual background other than to say that he has no formal credentials for his expertise; he is self-taught.

Snyder lives in Berkeley, California. He can be reached c/o RGE, 2000 Center Street, #1067, Berkeley, CA 94704.

## KEN USTON

Ken Uston is known in gambling circles as *Mr. Blackjack,* according to the Philadelphia Enquirer, and that title sits on his head like a crown!

Uston, brought up in a middle-class New York City household, graduated from Yale University with honors. Uston, who was awarded a Phi Beta Kappa key, then went on to Harvard Business School for his MBA.

At 31, he was earning $42,500 a year plus fringe benefits as a Senior Vice President of the Pacific Stock Exchange.

Over the years, he displayed not only an avid interest in the game of Blackjack, but, using his computer expertise, was winning more and more. He had a prestigious position, made an excellent living, and had an avocation that brought him a great deal of satisfaction. Then came that fateful telephone call from Al Francesco asking him if he would consider becoming a member of a Blackjack team. The rest is history.

Uston, a much sought after writer has authored *The Big Player* with R. Rapaport, and his best-seller, *Million Dollar Blackjack.* In addition, he has written many articles on the subject of Blackjack and has appeared on numerous radio and television shows.

In 1981, Uston was quoted as saying that he and his associates won in excess of four million dollars. When pressed further, he said that his best score was in Las Vegas, where he won $27,000 in forty-five minutes.

Just about every casino in the world has lost money to Ken Uston.

## D. H. MITCHELL

D. H. Mitchell is a pseudonym but Mitchell requests that his real identity remain a secret. He has a B.S. in Engineering from City College in New York, an M.A. in Mathematics from the University of Southern California, and a Ph.D. in Economics from Claremont Graduate School in Claremont, California.

Most of Mitchell's business experience has been in the field of Systems Analysis and Synthesis. Synthesis has to do with designing hardware and/or computer programs to perform desired tasks or functions in a reliable and cost-effective manner. Systems Analysis involves finding the shortcomings of existing hardware or software and finding ways to do the job better.

Mitchell, since reading Edward O. Thorp's book, *Beat the Dealer*, in 1971, has been researching a Blackjack system that can be used in both single-deck and multiple-deck play.

He has written numerous articles on the subject and has authored, *DHM Simplified Blackjack System*, 1974; *DHM Professional Blackjack System*, 1975; and *DHM Expert Blackjack System*, 1977. In addition, he presented a paper co-authored with Stanley Roberts at the Fourth Conference on Gambling held in Reno, Nevada.

Mitchell, who lives in Southern California, travels extensively and is a much sought after writer. He continues his work in the field of Systems Analysis and Synthesis.

# CHAPTER SIX

# BASIC STRATEGIES AND COMMON VARIATIONS

## PART I: BASIC STRATEGY

### by STANLEY ROBERTS

Basic strategy is the proper way to play your Blackjack hand *without card counting* using only the information about what your hand holds and what the dealer's face-up card is, under a given set of rules and number of decks. Basic strategy is *not* one set of rules for every Blackjack game played in any casino. The basic strategy rules you will use are determined by the number of decks in a game and the rules of the casino where you will play. In other words, usually every change in game conditions will prompt a change in basic strategy; however, there are rarely rule(s) changes when the number of decks is increased beyond four decks. In effect, there is no such thing as just one basic strategy for the game of Blackjack, but *many* basic strategies—one for each set of playing conditions.

If you learn the basic strategy rules for a single-deck game thoroughly, the changes for multiple-deck play and casino conditions shouldn't give you too much trouble.

To determine the proper strategy to use, a player should ask himself a series of questions. The first question is: "Do I have a SURRENDER hand?"

(If the casino you are in does not permit a particular rule, e.g., Surrender, then you should go on to the next question.)

If you will look at Table 6-1: SURRENDER—BASIC STRATEGY (SINGLE DECK), you will see that SURRENDER is your best play IF you hold a 10,6 and the dealer shows an ace. If the dealer shows a 10 and you have 10,6; or 10,5; or 9,7; or 9,6; or 7,7; you should SURRENDER since Surrender is your proper playing strategy. If you are holding any other cards, such as 5,5, then you continue on with your question-asking and decision-making.

Surrender is not a money-winning strategy *per se,* but a *money-saving* strategy. When used correctly, Surrender results in the loss of half your original wager, whereas without it, more than 75% of the time, *all* of your wager would be lost. So, in the long run, Surrender becomes a profitable play.

**TABLE 6-1**

| SURRENDER—BASIC STRATEGY (SINGLE DECK) | |
|---|---|
| DEALER SHOWS | YOU SURRENDER |
| Ace | (10,6) |
| 10 | (10,6), (10,5), (9,7) (9,6), or (7,7) |

If you do not have a Surrender hand, you go to the next question: "Do I have a PAIR?"

Table 6-2: PAIR SPLITTING—BASIC STRATEGY (SINGLE DECK) tells you when to split a pair. For example, if you have 6,6, and the dealer shows 2 or 3 or 4 or 5 or 6, split your pair of 6's. If the dealer shows any other card, do not split your pair of 6's.

Some casinos allow the player to double down after splitting a pair while others will only allow doubling on the first two cards dealt. The asterisk in Table 6–2 tells you those situations where doubling after a split is allowed (DASA). For example, if you are dealt a pair of 3's, Table 6–2 tells you to split them when the dealer

**TABLE 6-2**

| PAIR SPLITTING—BASIC STRATEGY (SINGLE DECK) | |
|---|---|
| YOUR HAND | DEALER SHOWS |
| (2,2) | 3-7 (*2-7) |
| (3,3) | 4-7 (*2-7) |
| (4,4) | Never (*4-6) |
| (5,5) | Never |
| (6,6) | 2-6 |
| (7,7) | 2-7 (*2-8) |
| (8,8) | Always |
| (9,9) | 2-9, Except 7 |
| (10,10) | Never |
| (Ace,Ace) | Always |

*Indicates when doubling after split is allowed (DASA)

is showing 4 through 7. But, if doubling after a split is allowed, then you can split your pair of 3's against the dealer's 2 through 7. If you get a good card (such as a 7 or an 8) on at least one of your hands, you will have a good doubling down situation.

Pairs should be resplit if possible. If you have a pair of 3's and your basic strategy rules say to split them and the dealer places another 3 on one of your split cards, that pair should be split again, and so on.

A pair of aces are treated differently in most casinos in that they cannot be resplit and only one card is dealt to each. Also, if a ten-value card is dealt to one or both of the split aces, you will *not* have a *natural,* you have a card total of twenty-one. If the hand wins (and it will if the dealer does not have a *natural*), you will receive even money instead of the 3-to-2 Blackjack payoff; nevertheless, aces should always be split.

If you don't have a Surrender hand or a pair that can be split, the third question you should ask is: "Do I have a SOFT DOUBLING hand?" (Remember, a *soft* hand is one that contains an ace and a card other than a ten; for example, an ace,6 is a *soft* seventeen.)

Table 6-3: SOFT DOUBLING—BASIC STRATEGY (SINGLE DECK) is read in the same manner as Table 6-2. That is, you look at your hand then at the dealer's card, and determine what your playing strategy should be. When would you double down with ace,7? You would double down if the dealer shows 3 or 4 or 5 or 6. If you have a *soft* hand, but Table 6-3 does not allow you to double down on it, you would go to Table 6-5 and use SOFT STANDING Strategy.

**TABLE 6-3**

| SOFT DOUBLING—BASIC STRATEGY (SINGLE DECK) | |
|---|---|
| YOUR HAND | DEALER SHOWS |
| (Ace,2); (Ace,3); (Ace,4); (Ace,5) | 4-6 |
| (Ace,6) | 2-6 |
| (Ace,7) | 3-6 |
| (Ace,8) | 6 |
| (Ace,9) | Never |

Let's assume for a moment that you don't have a Blackjack (an instant winner), or a hand that should be surrendered, or a pair that should be split,* or even a soft doubling hand. What is your next move? You ask yourself the next question: "Do I have a HARD DOUBLING hand?"

Table 6-4: HARD DOUBLING—BASIC STRATEGY (SINGLE DECK) is read in the same manner as the previous ones. You would double down on a hard total of *ten* IF the dealer shows 2 through 9.

**TABLE 6-4**

| HARD DOUBLING—BASIC STRATEGY (SINGLE DECK) | |
|---|---|
| YOUR HAND | DEALER SHOWS |
| (6,2) | Never |
| (5,3) or (4,4) | 5 or 6 |
| 9 | 2-6 |
| 10 | 2-9 |
| 11 | Always |

Table 6-4 is the one you should refer to after you have split a pair (DASA) and are contemplating doubling down on one or both of your hands. If hard doubling does not apply or is not allowed by this table (a hard total of nine versus the dealer's 10, for instance), then you would refer to Table 6-6, HARD STANDING Strategy.

---

*\*Pairs that should not be split will fall into HARD STANDING Strategy or HARD DOUBLING Strategy.*

Let's say that you were dealt an ace,6 (a SOFT hand) against a dealer's 7. According to Table 6–3, you can only double down if a dealer is showing a 2 through 6. What should you do? Ask yourself the next question: "Do I have a SOFT STANDING hand?"

Table 6-5: SOFT STANDING—BASIC STRATEGY (SINGLE DECK) tells you when to *hit* and when to *stand*. For example, if you have a soft hand of ace,6 and the dealer shows a 7, you would "hit" (take another card) until the soft total of your cards added up to eighteen or greater. Similarly, if you had an ace,7 and the dealer showed a 9 or 10, you would hit until your cards equaled nineteen or more. If Table 6-3 tells you that you do not have a SOFT DOUBLING hand,* than SOFT STANDING Strategy takes over.

**TABLE 6-5**

| SOFT STANDING—BASIC STRATEGY (SINGLE DECK) | |
| --- | --- |
| DEALER SHOWS | YOU STAND ON SOFT |
| 2-8 | 18 |
| 9 or 10 | 19 |
| Ace | 18 (*19) |
| *Indicates casino hits soft 17 (Ace,6), (Ace,2,4), etc. | |

*If SOFT DOUBLING is not allowed*, period, *as is the case in Reno, Nevada, then SOFT STANDING Strategy is used.*

NOTE: Some casinos require that their dealers stand on all seventeen point totals while other casinos require their dealers to hit a soft seventeen total. It's easy to tell what that particular casino's policy is—it is printed on the playing felt of the Black-jack table. In casinos where dealers hit a soft seventeen, the SOFT STANDING Strategy against a dealer's ace is for you, the player, to stand on nineteen rather than eighteen.

With your hand of ace,6 and following Table 6-5 (remember, the dealer shows a 7), you ask for a hit. If you draw a 4, you have a soft twenty-one, a probable winner. If you draw a 5, your hand is no longer soft. (The soft total for ace,6,5 would be twenty-two, a bust.) Now you have a *hard* twelve. Since your hand is no longer soft, you must now (and this is the final series of deci-sions) refer to Table 6-6.

Table 6-6: HARD STANDING—BASIC STRATEGY (SINGLE DECK) shows the most frequently used strategies in casino Black-jack. Pairs come only occasionally, as do hard and soft doubling hands. To be more precise, you will receive a pair 13.1% of the time in a single-deck game (14.5% in a four-deck game). But, not all of these pairs can be split. Seventy percent of the time, you will be faced with the simple-but-not-so-simple dilemma of whether to hit or stand.

**TABLE 6-6**

| HARD STANDING—BASIC STRATEGY (SINGLE DECK) | |
|---|---|
| DEALER SHOWS | YOU STAND ON |
| 2 or 3 | 13 |
| 4-6 | 12 |
| 7, 8, 9 or Ace | 17 |
| 10 | 17 or (7,7) |

Table 6-6 is followed in the same manner as the others. When a dealer is showing 2 or 3, you must hit your hand until your card total is thirteen or more. Similarly, if a dealer is showing a ten-value card, you will stand only if you have a total of seventeen or a pair of 7's. Remember, if Surrender is allowed, a pair of 7's should be surrendered to a dealer's 10. In casinos where Surrender is not allowed (and they are in the majority), you should stand on 7,7.

Generally speaking, it is very important that the tables be followed to the letter. In Table 6-4, HARD DOUBLING Strategy, your hand of 6,2 is never a doubling hand, while 5,3 and 4,4 sometimes are. In Table 6-6, HARD STANDING Strategy, your hand of 9,5 is not the same as 7,7 (a pair of 7's). With 9,5, you would hit your hand until you reached seventeen, but your hand of 7,7 would stand.

When should you take INSURANCE? Since you are not counting cards in Basic Strategy, insurance is a poor bet, and it should never be made. In a single deck of cards, there are sixteen ten-value cards and thirty-six cards that are not ten value. This makes the chances of any one being a 10 about 31%. Since insurance is paid at the rate of 2-to-1, a dealer would have to have a 10 as his hole card under the ace 33.33% of the time for insurance to be an even bet. If a dealer's ace and your two cards are subtracted from the 52 as non-tens, the percentage is still only 32.6%. Simply said, until card counting is employed, insurance is a losing bet.

To sum up, playing casino Blackjack involves a series of question-asking and decision-making considerations. During *each* hand, you must ask yourself these strategy questions *in order.*

1. Do I have a SURRENDER hand?
2. Do I have a PAIR?
3. Do I have a SOFT DOUBLING hand?
4. Do I have a HARD DOUBLING hand?
5. Should I stand on my SOFT STANDING hand?
6. What does my HARD STANDING Strategy tell me to do?

If you follow this outline for decision-making, there will not be one hand that cannot be played correctly according to Basic Strategy.

See Appendix A (starting on page 195) for the following Basic Strategy Tables:

1. Single Deck—Reno-Lake Tahoe Rules;
2. Double Deck, Four or More Decks (Nevada Rules)
3. Recap for Four or More Decks (with Single Deck and Double Deck Exceptions); and
4. Four or More Decks—Atlantic City Rules.

## PART II: COMMON VARIATIONS
## by JULIAN H. BRAUN
## THE DEALER'S HOLE CARD EXPOSED GAME

About twenty to twenty-five years ago, there were many casinos in Nevada who believed that even if the dealer's hole card were exposed, the casino would still have the advantage. At least one astute player managed to arrange a proposition game on this basis at the Flamingo Hotel; however, after the player won several thousand dollars the game was called off. Amazingly, a casino in Winnemucca regularly dealt such a game but with a $10 bet limit.

About seventeen years ago I computed the player's edge in the one-deck typical Las Vegas Strip game to be about 9.9% providing the player always knew the dealer's hole card and played optimally with this knowledge. My strategy data for this game were presented in the second edition of Edward Thorp's, *Beat the Dealer,* and Richard Epstein's, *Theory of Gambling and Statistical Logic.* This information was useful since the deck was frequently dealt out to the end in those days. Thus, when the deck ran out and the dealer had to reshuffle after having received his hole card, an expert card counter would know the dealer's hole card and could play such hands accordingly. Also, on occasion, the dealer's hole card might be inadvertently (or, in some cases, deliberately) exposed.

I then asked myself what if the casino were to regularly show the dealer's hole card, and to make it a fairer game, the dealer would win all ties. I found that the knowledgeable player would still win at a 2.1% rate. My data on this subject were presented in Epstein's book. Epstein made up a name for this game: Zweikartenspiel—German for two-card play.

In October of 1979, Vegas World decided to introduce this game with several rules modifications which would give the edge back to the casino. Bob Stupak of Vegas World copyrighted the name "Double Exposure 21" for his version of the game which presumably means that the several other casinos which have since introduced the game have to call it something else, such as "No Secrets Blackjack," "Naked 21," etc.

The popularity of this new Blackjack variation caught on quickly and as of April, 1980, Double Exposure Blackjack was being played in as many as nine casinos in and around Las Vegas.

The rules in effect at Vegas World are as follows:

1. The player always wins with a Blackjack, but he wins even money instead of 3-to-2.

2. An Ace of Spades and a Jack of Spades pays double.

3. The dealer wins all ties EXCEPT for Blackjack.

4. Pairs may be split, but resplitting is not allowed.

5. Doubling down on any two cards is allowed after pair splitting.

6. Dealer hits a soft seventeen.

7. Five decks of cards are used.

8. A total of 21 achieved with 6,7, and 8 of the same suit pays double.

With these rules and optimim Basic Strategy play, I estimate that the player is at a .5% advantage. The Basic Strategy for this game is summarized in Table 6-7.

(See Table 6-7 on following page)

## TABLE 6-7

### BASIC STRATEGY FOR 5 DECK "DOUBLE EXPOSURE" 21*

| DEALER'S 2 CARD TOTAL | DOUBLE-DOWNS HARD | DOUBLE-DOWNS SOFT | SPLIT PAIRS | HARD STAND AT OR ABOVE | SOFT STAND AT OR ABOVE |
|---|---|---|---|---|---|
| 4 | 10,11 | 18 | A,6-9 | 12 | 18 |
| 5 | 9-11 | 16-18 | A-3,6-9 | 12 | 18 |
| 6 | 9-11 | 13-18 | A-3,6-9 | 12 | 18 |
| 7 | 10,11 | | A,8 | 16 or 17** | 18 |
| 8 | 10,11 | | A,8,9 | 16 | 19 |
| 9 | 11 | | A | 16 | 19 |
| 10 | | | A | 15 | 19 |
| 11 | | | | 14 | 18 |
| 12 | 8-11 | 13-19 | A-4,6-9 | 12 | 18 |
| 13 | 8-11 | 13-20 | A-4,6-10 | 12 | 18 |
| 14 | 5-11 | 13-20 | A-4,6-10 | 12 | 18 |
| 15 | 5-11 | 13-20 | A4,6-10 | 12 | 18 |
| 16 | 5-11 | 13-20 | A-4,6-10 | 12 | 18 |
| 17 | | | 2,3,6-8 | 18 | 18 |
| 18 | | | 9 | 19 | 19 |
| 19 | | | | 20 | 20 |
| 20 | | | | 21 | 21 |
| Soft 12 | | | A | 13 | 19 |
| Soft 13 | 11 | | A | 13 | 19 |
| Soft 14 | 10,11 | | A | 12 | 19 |
| Soft 15 | 10,11 | | A,9 | 12 | 19 |
| Soft 16 | 10,11 | | A,8,9 | 12 | 19 |
| Soft 17 | | | A,8 | 18 | 18 |
| Soft 18 | | | | 19 | 19 |
| Soft 19 | | | | 20 | 20 |
| Soft 20 | | | | 21 | 21 |

*Copyright 1979 Vegas World
**There is very little difference in this case. Hit the 9,7 hard 16 versus dealer total of 7 for a very slight gain. Stand on other hard "16's," except the 8,8 which should be split. EXCEPTION: If you get an 8 on a split 8, hit it.

## BLACKJACK THE HOME GAME

The home game of Blackjack has grown in popularity by leaps and bounds. The basic rules of home Blackjack are:

1. Dealer wins all ties.
2. Dealer stands on all seventeens.
3. Blackjack pays 2:1 to the player.
4. Insurance is not offered as an option.
5. Doubling down and pair splitting are permitted.
6. One card only on split aces.
7. Single deck games only.

Basic Strategy is as follows:

If dealer shows 2, 3, 4, 5, or 6 STAND on HARD 12 or more. If dealer shows 7 or 8 STAND on 17 or more; HIT 16 or less. If dealer shows 9 STAND on 16 or more; HIT 15 or less. If dealer shows 10 STAND on 15 or more; HIT 14 or less. If dealer shows ace STAND on 18 or more; HIT 17 or less. HIT SOFT 17 always. STAND on SOFT 18 or better if dealer shows 2 through 7. HIT SOFT 18 and STAND on SOFT 19 if dealer shows 8, 9, 10, or ace. EXCEPTIONS: STAND on a pair of 7's versus dealer's 10. HIT 10,2 versus dealer's 2.

### DOUBLING DOWN

| IF YOU ARE HOLDING | DOUBLE DOWN IF DEALER SHOWS |
|---|---|
| 11 | Anything other than an ace |
| 10 | Anything other than ace, 10, 9 |
| 9 | 6, 5, 4 |
| SOFT 18 | 6, 5, 4 |
| SOFT 17 | 6, 5, 4 |
| SOFT 16 | 6, 5 |
| SOFT 15 | 6, 5 |
| SOFT 14 | 6, 5 |
| SOFT 13 | 6, 5 |

EXCEPTIONS: Holding 6,5 double down versus an ace
Holding 8,2 double down versus a 9.

## PAIR SPLITTING

Always split aces. Never split 10's or 5's.
Split 9's if dealer shows anything other than ace, 10, 9, 7.
Split 8's if dealer shows anything other than ace, 10, 9.
Split 7's if dealer shows 3, 4, 5, 6, 7.
Split 6's if dealer shows 3, 4, 5, 6.
Split 4's if dealer shows 5.
Split 3's if dealer shows 3, 4, 5, 6.
Split 2's if dealer shows 4, 5, 6.

The dealer advantage for this game is 7.0%
Additional rule: Player wins automatically if he makes FIVE cards without going over 21. If this rule is in force:
Holding a 4-card HARD total of 17 or 16, HIT if dealer shows an ace, 10, 9, 8, or 7. Holding a 4-card HARD total of 15 or less, HIT.

Holding a 3-card HARD total of 12, HIT if dealer shows a 2, 3, 7, 8, 9, 10, or ace. STAND against dealer's 4, 5, or 6. Do not split a pair of 2's.

# CHAPTER SEVEN

# HIGHER LEVELS OF PLAY SYSTEMS

## by DR. D. HOWARD MITCHELL and STANLEY ROBERTS

Of the many Blackjack systems being marketed, you might be wondering which, if any, is suited to your needs. The purpose of this chapter is to discuss the information that has been published about Blackjack systems and hopefully make it easier for you to make a choice.

Most of what has been written about Blackjack systems stresses system performance. This performance is usually measured by a computer simulation such as those performed by Julian Braun in his book, *The Development and Analysis of Winning Strategies for the Casino Game of Blackjack,* published in 1974. Computer simulations can provide much useful information, but they are not the whole story. For example, DHM Associates has developed the DHM Ultimate System. Its performance is the best any system can achieve in a *computer* simulation without trying to predict the order in which the cards will appear. As Dr. Edward O. Thorp noted in 1976 in an article he wrote for *Gambling and Society,* shuffling is an imperfect process and there are opportunities for gains if enough were known about the imperfections. But, we do not know how to achieve the *performance* potential of the DHM Ultimate System or any of the gains from knowledge of shuffling imperfections except by using a computer to keep track of each and every card dealt WHEN IT IS BEING DEALT.

Blackjack play, however, with a computer at your side has not been welcome in a casino since the Joint Computer Conference was held in the Fall of 1965. Thus, a number of systems are of no practical use if one wants to play Blackjack in a casino.

There are several powerful (and, in some cases, expensive) Blackjack systems that can be used in a casino that don't need a carry-along computer. However, only the Professional Level (and above) player can use such systems—and expensive or not, they can be cost-effective for a player at that level of play. Very few Blackjack players have the background and skills needed to benefit from such systems.

On the other hand, many Blackjack players would be much better off if they used a good Basic Strategy system rather than whatever system they're using now. In this chapter, we will classify Blackjack systems on the basis of their difficulty.

There are five levels of Blackjack play:
1. Basic Strategy—no counting.
2. Intermediate—a simple side count.
3. Advanced—a running count.
4. Professional—a true count plus an optional side count of aces.
5. Expert—anything more complicated than Professional.

## BASIC STRATEGY

Basic Strategy, which is covered in depth in Chapter Six, is the easiest to learn.

## INTERMEDIATE LEVEL

The only way you can do better at Blackjack when you are already using Basic Strategy is to add a count system that gives you some information about the distribution of cards which have been dealt. Very few players can remember the cards played so this is usually done with a card-counting system. Such a system tells the player how to adjust the betting and playing strategy using the information currently available about the composition of the deck (the cards which have not been dealt). With this information, you, the player, can adjust your betting action accordingly. (Chapter Fourteen discusses bankrolling and betting in greater depth.)

At the Intermediate Level that count system would be a simple one. The most popular Intermediate Level simple counting systems are Thorp's Five-Count; Revere's Five-Count; and Roberts' Five-Count, Six-Count and/or Ace Count.

The simplest and first published count was the Five-Count introduced by Dr. Edward O. Thorp in the first edition of his book, *Beat the Dealer.* This system involves counting only the number of fives the player has seen since the deck was last shuffled. When there are no more fives left in the deck (i.e., all four fives have been seen), the player bets more and changes his playing strategy. Thorp explained in this first edition of his book that his findings revealed that removing the four fives from an otherwise full deck gives the player an advantage of about 3.3%. When there are one or more fives in the deck (which is most of the time), the player then has little or no advantage.

When Thorp's book first appeared in 1962, dealers normally dealt the full deck. Now, the deck is usually shuffled long before the last card is reached so that the favorable situations upon which Thorp's system was based became relatively rare and today there is little gain to be realized from using his original Five-Count Strategy.

In the second edition of his book, Thorp suggested increasing the bet size whenever the number of fives left in the deck is below normal proportions and decreasing the bet size when the proportion is abnormally high. This betting strategy, in addition to the Five-Count, makes it a favorable option once again.

Revere's Five-Count system formalized Thorp's concept and was published in 1973 in his book, *Playing Blackjack as a Business.*

Stanley Roberts took a different tack in his book, *How to Win at Weekend Blackjack,* also published in 1973. His strategy included a Five- and Six-Count, and/or an Ace-Count. His findings were consistent with Thorp's findings that the removal of four fives has a more favorable effect on the player's chances than the removal of four cards of any other value. Removing four aces has a more unfavorable effect than removing four of any other face value cards from an otherwise full deck.

Roberts has recently refined and added to his Intermediate systems as published in his new book, *The Beginner's Guide to Winning Blackjack.*

## ADVANCED LEVEL

There are several card-counting systems available which are more advanced than a simple Five-Count.

Table 7-1 below lists the better Advanced Level systems. Unlike the Professional Level systems, the Advanced Level systems do not use any arithmetic beyond counting and comparing.

(See Table 7-1 on following page)

**TABLE 7-1**

## ADVANCED BLACKJACK SYSTEMS

| SYSTEM | COUNT | DECK FAVORABILITY |
|---|---|---|
| Roberts' Ten Count | +1 for 10's | very rich, rich, poor, very poor |
| Roberts' One-Number Conversion Supplement | −2 for 10's<br>+1 for non-tens | very rich, rich, poor, very poor |
| Revere Plus-Minus* | −1 for 10's & aces<br>+1 for 2-6's | count less than one, count one or more, two or more |
| DHM | −1 for 10's<br>+1 for 2-5's | negative, neutral, positive |
| Uston Plus-Minus | −1 for 10's & aces<br>+1 for 3-7's | plus count, minus count |

*Revere's Plus-Minus system is based on the Dubner High-Low Count used in a Professional Level system described by Thorp. In that system, aces are included in the high-card count.

Roberts' Ten-Count uses a count of tens seen and his One-Number Conversion Supplement counts the total cards seen. Because it is easier for most people to count up than down, both of these counts are simpler than Thorp's counts. In Roberts' system, you compare the number of cards seen with the "point of favorability" for the number of tens seen. If the number of cards seen is at least as large as the point of favorability, the tens left in the deck make up a more than normal proportion of the cards left and the deck is "rich"; therefore, the player should increase his unit bet.

The other Advanced Level systems use what is often called a *running count* to distinguish it from a *true count* which is used in Professional Level play.

The running count is the direct result of the card-counting operation without any further manipulations required to determine the true count. The other Advanced Level systems in Table 7-1 have you deduct one (-1) from the running count whenever you see a ten value card (10, Jack, Queen, or King) and add one (+1) whenever you see one of the cards designated in the second group for that system.

An Advanced Level system not included in Table 7-1 is the Austin Starter System. This system which is based on Charles Einstein's High-Low Count (from his book, *How to Win at Blackjack*), is not included because it uses the Einstein count for bet variation only. Thus, the significant gains that would accrue from proper use of this count are lost. Briefly, the Einstein count omits the aces from the high group and the deuces from the low group.

There has been a fair amount of controversy about whether 3–6 as a low group is better than 2–5. However, our studies have shown that there is no practical difference in performance between either low group. The theoretical calculations actually show 2–5 to be better by 0.001%.

## PROFESSIONAL LEVEL

A number of systems for Professional Level Blackjack players have been developed since the early sixties. All of these systems use at least one *true* count.

An important advantage of grouping the systems into classes is that there is very little difference in performance between the better systems within each class. This holds true except for those systems in the Expert Level class. However, there are other differences between these systems which tend to make some systems harder to use than others even though they all belong to the same class.

The most important difference has to do with the need for division by a fraction. Many people have difficulty dividing fractions. For example, the HI-OPT system, listed in Table 7-2, recommends that you divide the running count by ¾ when ¼ of the deck has been played.

(See Table 7-2 on following page)

## TABLE 7-2

## PROFESSIONAL BLACKJACK SYSTEMS

| Date | System | Division by Fraction | High Group | Point Value | Low Group | Point Value | Ace Count |
|------|--------|---------------------|-----------|-------------|-----------|-------------|-----------|
| 1962 | Thorp Ultimate | Yes | 9,10,ace | -3,-7,-9 | 2-7 | +4,+5,+6 | No |
| 1963 | Dubner* | No | 10,ace | -1 | 2-6 | +1 | No |
| 1966 | Collver | Yes | 10 | -⅔ | 2-9 | ⅓ | Bet |
| 1968 | Einstein, Charles | Yes | 10 | -1 | 3-6 | +1 | Bet |
| 1971 | Revere Advanced Point Count | Yes | 9,10,ace | -1,-3,-4 | 2-7 | +2,+3,+4 | No |
| 1973 | Revere Advanced Point Count | Yes | 9,10 | -2,-3 | 2-7 | +1,+2,+3,+4 | Bet |

| Year | Name | | | | | | |
|---|---|---|---|---|---|---|---|
| 1974 | DHM Professional | No | 10 | −1 | 2-5 | +1 | Bet & Play |
| 1974 | HI-OPT | Yes | 10 | −1 | 3-6 | +1 | Mostly Bet |
| 1976 | HI-OPT II | Yes | 10 | −2 | 2-7 | +1,+2 | Mostly Bet |
| 1977 | Wong High Low | Yes | 10,ace | −1 | 2-6 | +1 | Bet |
| 1977 | Uston Advanced Point Count | Yes | 10, 9 | −3,−1 | 2-7 | +1,+2,+3 | Mostly Bet |
| 1979 | Canfield Master System | Yes | 9,10 | −1,−2 | 2-7 | +1,+2 | No |
| 1981 | Snyder Zen Count | Yes | 10,ace | −2,−1 | 2-7 | +1,+2 | No |

*Also used by Patterson, Braun and Wong.

Thorp's Ten Count and the first four systems in Table 7-2 are of historical interest only. The early systems were quite crude by modern standards because their developers were not using any of the more powerful optimization techniques now available. The Einstein system of 1968 can be regarded as a prototype for the HI-OPT System. The Collver system (*Scientific Blackjack & Complete Casino Guide* by Donald L. Collver) is noted only because he had a more advanced version that is somewhat similar to two Expert Level systems.

The systems which use only a plus one (+1) value for the low group and a minus one (−1) value for the high group are obviously much easier to learn and use than those systems which have more levels to contend with. Braun found that there was no significant difference in system performance between HI-OPT and the Revere Advanced Point Count. Yet, the former uses only plus one (+1) and minus one (−1) while the latter has −3, −2, 0, 1, 2, 3, and 4. The problems Ken Uston had in mastering the Revere Advanced Point Count are covered in his book, *The Big Player.*

All of the newer Professional Level systems offer an optional side count of aces. This recognizes the fact that the role of aces in a betting strategy differs from its optimal role in a playing strategy. Thus, the formal definition of the Professional Level systems are those systems which have one true count and at most one side count.

The first system which used more complicated counts than the above definition was Thorp's Ultimate System (*Beat the Dealer,* 1962 edition). This system used a point-count for bet variation in addition to Thorp's Ten-Count for playing decisions. Thorp estimated that by dealing down to the last card, his Ultimate Strategy would win at one and a half to two times the rate of the Ten-Count alone. Yet, it was relegated to only a footnote in the second edition of his book. His Ultimate Strategy was used as the basis for various point-count systems such as Revere's, HI-OPT II, and Uston's—all three listed in Table 7-3.

Many other point count systems have appeared in the past few years. However, there is no evidence that any of them is superior to those listed in Table 7-2.

## EXPERT LEVEL

The systems more complicated than the Professional Level which have appeared in publications since Thorp's Ultimate Strategy are summarized in Table 7-3.

The first three systems in Table 7-3 all divide the deck into the same groups of cards. The card-counting methods differ and the ways in which these methods are used differ. Collver used a relatively cumbersome way to count the cards and he did not have the benefit of any of the modern system-optimization tools. Thus, he was not able to follow through on what proved to be a very good concept up to that point.

(See Table 7-3 on following page)

## TABLE 7-3

### EXPERT BLACKJACK SYSTEMS

| Date | System | # of Counts True | Side | High | Groups Low | Other |
|------|--------|------|------|------|------|-------|
| 1966 | Collver Advanced | 2 | 1 | 10 | 2-5 | ace,6-9 |
| 1975 | Fristedt & Heath | 2 | 1 | 10 | 2-5 | ace,6-9 |
| 1976 | HI-OPT/Multiple Parameters | 1 | 5 | 10 | 3-6 | ace,2,7,8,9 |
| 1977 | Sklansky Key Card | 0 | 10 | 10 | | ace,2,3,4,5,6,7,8,9 |
| 1978 | DHM Ultimate | 2 | 10 | 10 | | ace,2,3,4,5,6,7,8,9 |

Bert Fristedt and David Heath devised the Fristedt and Heath system first published in May, 1977, in *Winning* magazine. The title of that article was, "The Most Powerful Blackjack Strategy Ever Devised." The manner in which they portrayed their system in this article was very effective, but it is completely impractical for casino play. Furthermore, their presentation indicates that their optimization was less complete and less accurate than the techniques used to develop other Expert Level systems. Fristedt & Heath use the Ace Count only for betting; it is not integrated into the playing strategy.

The Multiple Parameters for HI-OPT represent an entirely different approach to a Blackjack system. The mathematical foundation for that approach was laid out in a paper by Peter Griffin first presented at the First Conference on Gambling. His paper presented at the Second Conference on Gambling gave the approach itself. The key point in this system was to have a separate side count for each card value not in the true count. For HI-OPT that means a separate side count for ace, 2, 7, 8, and 9. For HI-OPT II, the side counts are for ace, 8, and 9. Griffin maintains that you gain a 0.2% advantage when you use his side counts as opposed to a side count of aces alone. To achieve this 0.2% gain, the tables to be memorized and used in the decision-making strategy for casino play are larger and more complicated than those which make up the system without the extra side counts. In view of this added complexity, other Expert Level systems would be easier to learn and to use.

The Sklansky Key Card concept ("Getting the Best of It: The Key Card Concept—An Extra Edge at the Blackjack Table," *Gambling Times,* August, 1977) is recommended as an addition to a Basic Strategy and only a few rules for using the ten side counts need to be memorized. Since there are expert bridge players who can keep track of every card in the deck, the system is probably a feasible one.

The DHM Ultimate System was inspired by the Sklansky Key Card concept. If you are going to go to the trouble of counting each card value separately, you should do something useful with the information. The best approach would be to program a computer to use all ten of the side counts to evaluate the possible alternatives and tell you which is best. Unfortunately, computers are not welcome in casinos. Thus, the DHM Ultimate system is an academic device only to find out how close to this ultimate performance the DHM Expert system comes. (The DHM Expert system is not covered in this chapter since it has not been published and is only available on a private lesson basis.)

# CHAPTER EIGHT

# CASINO CUSTOMS

## by ARNOLD SNYDER

### RULES FOR DEALERS

Dealers are always subject to the customs of the house. In Chapter Four, rules were described as they pertain to the playing decisions of the game of Blackjack. These are the rules which any dealer will explain to anyone who wants to play.

Of greater importance are the various house customs which a casino explains in detail to its dealers and gaming personnel only. You can learn some of these customs by observation. Some, you can only surmise.

The following rule is an example of customary procedure which would be of critical importance to a card counter: Any time any player more than doubles his last bet, shuffle the cards. There are few casinos that follow this custom religiously, but there are many that would follow it for certain players; such as players unknown to the house, players making large bets or players under suspicion of card counting. Some casinos require all dealers to shuffle before any sizable portion of the cards have been played. This game would be a waste of time for a card counter. You must see a sizable proportion of the cards before your card counting will begin to pay off. Casinos that do not allow dealers to deal deeply into the deck should be avoided.

Most casinos are cautious with unknown players, especially with high bettors. Once you convince them you are not a card counter, conditions should loosen. Whether or not it would be worth your time to cultivate a non-counter act for a counter-paranoid location depends on how much time you expect to play in that casino. If you play many hours per week, developing new locations will be worth your effort. If you only visit casinos once or twice a year, you're better off seeking casinos which are not as paranoid about card counters in the first place.

Another custom which you will encounter in every casino is the card-burning procedure. Many years ago all dealers burned one card by turning it upside down and placing it on the bottom of the deck so that the players would not be able to see the bottom card as the cards were dealt. Thus, burning a card served a purpose in a single-deck game.

There are now dozens of variations of this card-burning practice. Although burning a card serves no purpose whatsoever in a shoe game (except to foil card counters), cards are still burned and sometimes overzealously. You'll find dealers who will burn anywhere from 1 to 10 cards off the top, and some will burn a card between every hand. Some casinos may practice such enthusiastic card burning only against unknown players, or suspected counters. Some casinos, as standard policy, may burn cards with relish.

In one sense, card burning is similar to early shuffling. It prohibits the card counter from obtaining as much information about the remaining cards as possible. In another sense, card burning can be even more devastating to the card counter. A dealer who burns cards zealously will appear to be dealing out a more sizable proportion of cards than in reality he is. This will give card counters a false optimism about how loose the game is, and will likely cause them to overbet in less-than-favorable situations.

Some casinos allow dealers to keep their own tokes (i.e., tips or winnings from bets placed for the dealer by a player). Some casinos require dealers to pool their tokes and divide them up equitably. In this way, dealers who get stuck at tables with non-tippers won't suffer. A significant amount of a dealer's income comes from tokes. Dealers who keep their own tokes may be inclined to *hustle* tokes. This can be bothersome. On the other hand, dealers may occasionally be found who will be *influenced* by tokes. Perhaps they will deal deeper or will ignore your betting spread if you place an occasional bet for them.

Most players should not attempt toking dealers for *favors*. This is dangerous. Reading dealers is an art which some players never acquire. Only very experienced players can take advantage of dealers who would be influenced by tokes. Most card counters would toke away all their potential profits. An occasional small toke for the dealer, if you are winning, may be considered adequate. Do not expect favors. Hopefully, the dealer will not suspect you of being a counter.

Generally, dealers who hustle tokes would tend to be in the less opulent casinos. Card counters tend to classify casinos as either *sawdust joints* or *carpet joints* referring, of course, to the floor covering. Actually, you're not likely to find sawdust on any casino's floor, as many sawdust joints, in fact, are carpeted.

## THE ATMOSPHERE—SAWDUST AND CARPETS

As a rule, card counters are generally better off in carpet joints for a number of reasons. First of all, if you are serious about making money at Blackjack, you will probably be placing some serious bets. Casinos which have maximum betting limits of $1000 or more will not pay as much attention to you as a casino with a $50 or a $100 table limit if you're making frequent bets of $50 or $100.

In sawdust joints, there are few "comps." Since table limits are low, these casinos cannot afford to pay for your room (if they have rooms), or to pay for your airfare, or even your dinner. In a carpet joint high rollers are sometimes treated like royalty because the casino hopes to make everything back (and then some) at the tables. In a sawdust joint, a high roller is not trusted. "Why would someone with so much money play in a sleazy pit like this?" A sawdust floorman might wonder.

If you play for high stakes, then you must stick to casinos where your action is affordable. Likewise, you must blend in with other high rollers according to dress, grooming, manners, etc. American casinos do not post formal dress rules, but the unwritten rule is that you must look like you can afford your own bets.

Another reason why card counters sometimes avoid sawdust joints in Nevada is that counters are more suspicious of small casinos being places where outright cheating may be house policy. The Nevada Gaming Commission will revoke the license and prosecute without hesitation any casino it believes to be cheating the public at the games it offers. Casinos must play by the rules.

The card counter's viewpoint is this: If a casino has a hundred Blackjack tables, it will employ virtually thousands of dealers, pit bosses, etc., over the years. Such a casino cannot chance that some of these employees will not become disgruntled at various times. A single dealer could blow the whistle and bring the roof down on a billion dollar enterprise. Such a casino cannot afford to instruct its dealers to cheat. But what about a casino with only a few Blackjack tables. For all you know, this casino is a "family" operation. They may have employed the same half-dozen dealers for ten years. Such an operation could conceivably get away with illegal activities indefinitely. It's just a small circle of friends.

The reality is this: Cheating dealers do exist, but, in my opinion, you are probably as likely to encounter them in carpet joints as in sawdust joints. Why? Because the problem with cheating is not so much that the house policy is to cheat, but that individual dealers may be cheating for their own gain, unbeknownst to the house. Why in carpet joints? Because that's where the high rollers are. If you had spent years of your life practicing to perfection certain sleight-of-hand card tricks which could land you in prison, would you seek a job in some sawdust joint where you might have to perform your tricks 50 times per shift to make your talent worthwhile? Or, would you find a carpet job where you would have to perform your sleight-of-hand tricks only once or twice per shift for some wild-betting, half-drunk high roller?

Protecting yourself against a cheating dealer should concern not only card counters but all Blackjack players. Such a dealer can decimate your bankroll in no time. It is very difficult to detect legerdemain in the hands of a master of this art. If you suspect you are being cheated, leave the table. Do not continue to play "until you're sure." Do not alert the dealer or floorman that you suspect cheating. Cheating is a very serious charge and you will likely have no proof.

Cheating is not common. Ninety-nine plus percent of the dealers follow house rules to the letter. Don't become paranoid that you're being cheated every time you're on a losing streak. Even for the most expert card counter, the advantage over the house is small. Normal fluctuation will cause almost as many losing streaks as winning streaks. So, continuous losses over many months may be indicative of neither normal fluctuations, nor poor card-counting technique, nor cheating.

Half the Blackjack games in this country cannot be beaten by ANY card-counting system. This is due to table conditions. How do you judge table conditions for profitability? This is not easy, but certain guidelines will help.

First, seek uncrowded tables. If the tables are full (five to seven players per table), don't expect much action. Your best bet is to wait until the crowds are gone. When many players are at the table, you will play very slowly. Thus, even if you play a winning game, you will win slowly.

Next, choose the game with the fewest number of decks.

The effect of multiple-deck games is far more drastic to the card counter than to the basic strategy player. If a casino offers two-, four-, and six-deck games, by all means play at the two-deck tables.

But, you might ask, what if the two-deck games are crowded, and the four- and six-deck games are not? My answer is that it is very difficult to get any notable long-run advantage in a six-deck game (without the "Early Surrender" rule). But, you may be better off in a head-to-head, four-deck game than in a crowded two-deck game simply because you might play two to three times faster when the table is uncrowded, and your betting may be more accurate. Actually, the best approach for crowded multi-deck games may be table hopping and playing only when the count is favorable. These are hard games to beat.

Seek games in which a sizable proportion of the cards are dealt out between shuffles. A two-deck game with only 50% (one deck) of the cards dealt out is usually less profitable than a four-deck game with 75% (or three decks) dealt out. Generally, if the dealer does not deal out at least 60% of the cards, the profit potential for a card counter will be small, if it, indeed, exists at all.

One casino countermeasure which you should watch out for is *preferential shuffling by count.* Casino slang for this practice is "percentaging" the player. A casino is said to percentage the player when they employ card-counting dealers who will deal out the "negative" decks, and shuffle away the "positive" ones.

Thus far, the legality of this practice has not been tested in the Nevada courts. Various casinos do it more or less blatantly, and technically, it may be legal. For the card counter, it is quite obvious when a casino is percentaging. Naturally, a counter is advised to leave such a table. Non-card-counting Blackjack players will not even be aware of this tactic. Too bad. It will prove quite costly to them.

Casinos which practice percentaging would argue that if card counting is legal for players, then it is likewise legal for casinos. The rules of the game are followed to the letter. Only the shuffling, which is traditionally at the casino's whim, is affected. The gaming public might retort that percentaging is a subtle form of cheating, since the casino by law must offer a game based on random order. Percentaging, as its name implies, extracts an extra percentage of the players' money via a non-random shuffling procedure which puts the odds in the house's favor.

## HISTORICAL REPUTATION

Traditionally, casinos have always made their money by offering *unfair* games; i.e., all casino games have always been *fixed* in favor of the house. Roulette, for instance, has a fixed house advantage of about 5.26% that no system can beat—only, occasionally, luck.

The line between a *game* and a *swindle* is sometimes very thin in a casino. The line between *doing business with you* and *giving you the business* is a question of phrasing. Casino gamblers have always accepted this as the price of the games. Card counters refuse to accept this.

Whether or not casinos will continue to offer a game such as Blackjack which can be beaten by skill remains to be seen. In my opinion, casino management is too intelligent to let Blackjack profits die. Casinos have thrived in the past two decades primarily because of the media attention to Blackjack systems. Ironically, no casino game is a bigger money-maker for the casinos than Blackjack, the one game that can be beaten by skill. Big money is drawn to the Blackjack tables because people want to try their "skill." Most people with money are not gamblers—which is why they have money. But these same people are more than willing to take a sporting risk on what may be a lucrative proposition. Blackjack attracts people to the tables who never play any other casino games. These are canny business people who are accustomed to taking money risks.

It's only a matter of time before these big money players learn the facts. In my opinion, if the casinos take away the possibility of profit from the game of Blackjack, they will, in the long run, be the biggest losers. The game will become just another gamble, and a lot of big money will go back to the commodities market and myriad other high-risk investments where speculators have fun and lose fortunes.

If some casinos continue to offer beatable Blackjack games, then those casinos with good games will thrive. Card counters, who are among the biggest spenders and most consistent customers of any casino, will patronize those casinos which offer the best games. These casinos will profit immensely. Like any high-risk investors, only a small fraction of card counters is good enough to make money.

When I walk into any major Nevada casino on a weekend night, I'll find fifty to a hundred Blackjack tables open—all of them full. These tables will remain open and full for some eight to ten hours with some 300 to 500 Backjack players wagering at any given moment in each casino. By standing behind the players and counting down the cards as they are played, I can usually spot a blatant card counter within ten minutes. The obvious betting and playing styles give them away. I recently surveyed three large Nevada casinos. I estimated that close to one out of every twelve players is a blatant card counter. Yet, in about four hours, I did not witness a single incident of any player being barred. I doubt many of these counters received much heat at all that night though most of them will undoubtedly get heat sometime. I'm sure that if I can spot them easily, so can the eye-in-the-sky (casino personnel using closed circuit television equipment). Casino management is aware of how much of its business (and profits) come from inept card counters. If the casinos gave heat to every counter they saw, they'd be continuously barring someone at every other table, all night long. But the majority of these blatant counters had one thing in common—they were long run losers. In all three casinos I surveyed, because of the crowds, the conditions were unbeatable. The shuffle points weren't deep enough. The betting was too inaccurate. The counters were sloppy in their decisions, even though they were so obviously counting. Many of these players would likely get barred quickly if they actually started playing in beatable games. Even in lousy games, these players won't last forever. They will be harrassed repeatedly because casinos don't like to tolerate break-even players, let alone winners.

There are now dozens of gambling publications which offer more and more accurate "inside" information on Blackjack—

including a growing number of newsletters specifically aimed at card counters. Most of these publications use various methods of rating the casinos' profitability according to conditions and reports of readers' experiences.

# CHAPTER NINE

# CASINO CONDITIONS

## by JERRY L. PATTERSON

### THE REAL WORLD OF CASINO PLAY

As a Blackjack practitioner, you should only be interested in Blackjack theory that can be turned into practical, profitable casino methods. This philosophy has been the foundation of success for both professional Blackjack players as well as the operators of franchised Blackjack schools and clinics.

This chapter will adhere to the philosophy of stressing the practical aspects of casino Blackjack play. We will discuss tips that you can use right now, not esoteric mathematical or computer studies that have no practical value inside the casino. You will learn how to evaluate a casino based on the impact on your bottom line, and not on whether or not you can pick up an extra 0.14% by being allowed to double down after splitting pairs.

There is a factor that has too long been overlooked in the real world of casino play—*The Shuffle*. This factor is called a super factor in the TARGET Instructional Program. The importance of the shuffle cannot be underestimated in evaluating a casino or a Blackjack table. To understand this, consider that Blackjack has been played on computers ever since card counting was invented in 1961. Hundreds of millions of hands have been played under ideal conditions with a perfect random shuffle. Unfortunately, a random shuffle just does not exist in the real world of casino play. To my knowledge a non-random or "real" shuffle has never been programmed on a computer. Blackjack computer studies are all based on something that does not exist—a random shuffle! We are not implying that card counting does not work—obviously, it does, and this has been proven many times over in the "real" world as well as the "theoretical" world. It has been published elsewhere that it takes 28 times to randomly shuffle a single deck of cards. Can you imagine how many times it would take to randomly shuffle six or eight decks of cards? This is just not possible in the real world.

We are going to give you some tips about the shuffle that could save or make you thousands of dollars or even tens of thousands of dollars depending on your bankroll. Let's start with this one. I have been asked hundreds of times over the past five years why so many card counters lose their bets in high count situations. When the count is high, the player has the advantage and should win his fair share of the hands. Why then do some experienced players lose five hands in succession when the count is extremely high? There is a very valid reason for this phenomenon and that is the possibility that the player was playing into a dealer bias which can exist on extremely high counts. This can happen because of card clumps produced by the "wash" (the first shuffle of fresh decks of cards) or the shuffle. Card clumps are not necessarily favorable to the card counter. Low card clumps can produce extremely high count situations. If the clump is big enough, you may never see the high cards which are "supposed" to come out. They may be behind the cut card. Thus, you are playing into low cards, which are favorable to the dealer, and losing. High card clumps can also hurt you. How many times have you waited patiently for a high count to develop only to see it dissipated on one hand of mainly 20's and Blackjacks? You may not even get one! The Tip: Don't play in these games. Leave the table. The non-random shuffle doesn't necessarily break up these clumps. Find a table with a better distribution of cards—especially if you're not winning.

The Tip described above is part of a new technique called TARGET. Using the tip should start you looking at Backjack tables with an entirely new perspective. That is the purpose of this chapter. Card-counting techniques still represent the fundamentals of winning at Blackjack. But, card counting combined with TARGET makes a very powerful winning technique. For example, it is known that card counting techniques yield only about 6 to 8% big bet opportunities. The TARGET player does not accept this and looks for other big bet opportunities engendered by powerful player biases. What produces these player biases: the wash and shuffle.

You will be introduced to the TARGET program in this chapter. Much of the data is just too sensitive to set forth in public print. If you would like more information about TARGET, you may contact me at the address given in Chapter Five.

## HOW TO EVALUATE A CASINO

For too long Blackjack books and Blackjack articles have recommended evaluating casinos according to the favorability of their rules of play. We are referring to rules such as: when you can double down, when you can double after splitting, when you can resplit pairs, etc. Most of these rules give you just a fraction of a percent additional advantage. There is certainly nothing wrong with this but you want to keep it in a proper perspective. There are other factors that are more important in casino evaluation: the shuffle, deck penetration, and heat.\*The most important rule of play is how many decks are in the game. A single-deck game is preferred over a two-deck game. A two-deck game is preferred over a shoe game.

You evaluate the shuffle based on whether or not it is "trackable." We will get into "shuffle-tracking" a little later in this chapter. I will teach you a simple shuffle-tracking technique. Other evaluation factors are part of the TARGET program

---

\**See Table 9-2.*

and are too sensitive to discuss in print.

There is an easy way to evaluate deck penetration. Use the following table:

**TABLE 9-1**

| EVALUATING DECK PENETRATION | |
|---|---|
| No. of decks in game | Decks dealt before shuffle |
| 1 | 3/4s (you must get at least 4 rounds) |
| 2 | 1.5 |
| 4 | 3 |
| 6 | 4 |
| 8 | 6 |

Heat is easy to evaluate. Is the pit boss or floor person noticing your play? Is your bet spread too high for the casino's comfort? You don't want to jeopardize your playing career in any one casino so limit your playing time and watch your betting spread. Don't play more than one hour in a casino and keep your betting spread from 4 to 1 in a single-deck game, 8 to 1 in a double-deck game and 12 to 1 in a shoe game, and you shouldn't have any problem. The tips below go into these factors in more detail.

## TABLE 9-2
## CASINO EVALUATION REPORT

### ATLANTIC CITY CASINOS

| NAME | NO. OF TABLES | SHUFFLE | DECK PENETRATION | DECKS | HEAT |
|------|---------------|---------|------------------|-------|------|
| Resorts | 84 | | .75+ | 6/8 | N |
| Bally's | 76 | T | .75+ | 8 | N |
| Trop | 76 | | .75+ | 6 | Y |
| Harrah's | 60 | | .75 | 8 | N |
| Playboy | 60 | | .75 | 8 | N |
| Sands | 59 | | .75+ | 8 | N |
| Nugget | 57 | | .75 | 8 | Y |
| Caesars | 56 | T | .75+ | 8 | N |
| Claridge | 34 | T | .75 | 6 | Y |

### LAS VEGAS STRIP CASINOS*

| NAME | NO. OF TABLES | SHUFFLE | DECK PENETRATION | DECKS | HEAT |
|------|---------------|---------|------------------|-------|------|
| Stardust | 48 | | | 1/2/6 | N |
| Holiday | 36 | | .75 | 1/2/6 | Y |
| L.V. Hilton | 36 | | .75 | 2/4 | Y |
| Riviera | 34 | | | 2/4 | Y |

| | | | | | |
|---|---|---|---|---|---|
| Frontier | 33 | | | 6 | N |
| Aladdin | 32 | | | 5 | |
| Desert Inn | 32 | | .67 | 6 | |
| Sahara | 32 | | | 2/5 | |
| El Rancho | 31 | | | 6 | |
| Maxim | 31 | | .75 | 1/2/4 | N |
| IP | 31 | | .75 | 2/6 | N |
| Sands | 24 | T | .75 | 2/4/6 | Y |
| Barbary | 23 | | .67 | 2/6 | Y+ |
| Marina | 22 | | | 5 | |
| Hacienda | 20 | | | 2/5 | N |
| Slots A Fun | 18 | | | 1/4 | N |
| Slipper | 17 | | | 6 | N |
| Castaways | 16 | | | 6 | N |
| Landmark | 15 | | | 1/4 | |
| Westward Ho | 15 | | | 1/6 | |
| Continental | 14 | | | 6 | |

*based on information available January, 1984.
Legend: Y+ = Extreme Heat; () in 1 deck games = no. of rounds before shuffle in head to head game with reasonable (2 to 4 to 1) spread; or .x−.y = % of cards dealt before shuffle.
    T = Trackable.

## TABLE 9-2 (continued)
## CASINO EVALUATION REPORT

| NAME | NO. OF TABLES | SHUFFLE | DECK PENETRATION | DECKS | HEAT |
|------|---------------|---------|------------------|-------|------|
| Royal | 9 | | | 1/5 | |
| King 8 | 7 | T | .90 | 4 | N |
| Nob Hill | 7 | | .60 | 1/2 | N |
| Ambassador | 6 | | | 4 | |

### LAS VEGAS DOWNTOWN CASINOS*

| NAME | NO. OF TABLES | SHUFFLE | DECK PENETRATION | DECKS | HEAT |
|------|---------------|---------|------------------|-------|------|
| 4 Queens | 36 | T | | 2/6 | Y |
| Nugget | 36 | | | 1/2/6 | N |
| Mint | 36 | | | 1/2/6 | Y |
| Fremont | 32 | T | | 1/2/6 | Y |
| Horseshoe | 32 | | .5 | 1/2/4 | N |
| Sundance | 28 | | | 2/4 | |
| Union Plaza | 28 | | | 2/5 | |
| Lady Luck | 18 | | | 1/7 | |
| Calif. | 16 | | | 2/6 | |
| Golden Gate | 16 | | | 1/2/4/5 | Y |

| | | .5 | 6 | |
|---|---|---|---|---|
| Las Vegas | 16 | | 6 | N |
| El Cortez | 12 | | 1/2 | Y+ |
| Orbit | 7 | | 4 | |

## RENO CASINOS*

| | | .5 | 6 | |
|---|---|---|---|---|
| MGM | 89 | .6 | 4 | |
| Harrah's | 87 | | 1 | |
| Circus | 62 | .7-1.0 | 1 | N |
| Harold's | 49 | .7 (4-5) | 1/2/4 | N |
| Reno Hilton | 39 | .6 | 1/2 | Y |
| Cal-Neva | 33 | .6 | 1/2 | |
| Peppermill | 25 | | 1/2 | |
| Eldorado | 25 | | 1/2 | N |
| Ramada | 19 | | 1/2/3 | |
| Comstock | 17 | .7-.9-1.0(6) | 1 | N |
| Fitzgerald's | 17 | | 1/2 | Y |
| Sundowner | 17 | .7-1.0 (5-8) | 1 | Y+ |
| Nevada | 14 | .6-.8 (3-4) | 1 | N |
| Onslow | 10 | .7 (4-6) | 1 | |

*based on information available January, 1984.
Legend: Y+ = Extreme Heat; () in 1 deck games = no. of rounds before shuffle in head to head game with reason-able (2 to 4 to 1) spread; or .x−.y = % of cards dealt before shuffle.
T = Trackable.

# PRACTICAL TIPS TO ENHANCE YOUR CASINO PLAY

## BLACKJACK TIP #1: INSURANCE AND OTHER PLAY VARIATIONS IN A FACE DOWN GAME (FOR CARD COUNTERS ONLY)

Assume here that you are using a system where tens and other high cards are counted as -1 and low cards are counted as +1.

When you take Insurance in a face-down game you need all the information you can get, right now, in the split second or two that you are allotted to make the Insurance decision. The problem that confronts you is that you might have a very high running count or true count, sufficient to make the insurance decision, but there are many unseen cards on the table that will influence your count. You must adjust your count for as many of these unseen cards as you possibly can. The first thing that you do is look at the cards of the players on either side of you. Adjust your count accordingly. The second thing you do is deduce the other players' unseen cards. If another player has tucked his two cards under his chips, that means he is standing and probably has a pat hand. You can assume that the count of that hand is -1. If a player takes Insurance on the pat hand, you can assume that he probably has a 20 and assign a tentative count, for Insurance purposes, of -2. If a player is holding his two cards in his hand, you can assume that he has either a hitting hand or stiff hand and the safest count to assign is 0. On the other hand, if a player who is holding his two cards takes Insurance, you can assume that he probably has a 10 or 11 and assign his hand a value of +1. All of these deductions must be made very quickly while the dealer is calling for Insurance. With a little practice, however, you will be surprised at how quickly you can figure up this "temporary" count. To get the necessary practice, set up a home game and instruct the other players in terms of what you want them to do.

Remember to return to your "true" running count after you have made the Insurance decision.

You have a little more time to deduce these unseen cards when making normal play variations. For example, suppose you have a 12 vs. 3 and you are attempting to decide whether to hit or stand. The index value for this decision is +2. You have a +3 but you must adjust this for the unseen cards. Do it the same way as above for the pat hands. If a player draws a card or two you can assume that the value of his two unseen cards is at least +1. If a player draws two or three cards to a standing hand, you can deduce that the value of his unseen cards is +2. Add the value of these unseen cards to your running count, make your hitting or standing decision, and then revert back to your "true" running count.

### BLACKJACK TIP #2: THE DOUBLE PEEK

The Double Peek is the easiest kind of dealer "tell" to detect. A tell is a subconscious body movement made by the dealer that will tip you off about the value of his or her hole card. Some dealers move differently or exhibit different body mannerisms when they are pat than they do when they are stiff. This information is invaluable and can be used to obtain a very healthy advantage of 2% or more if you can read the value of every hole card.

A Double Peek does not occur very often but when it does, you should use the information. The dealer, with a face card showing, peeks at the hole card; the dealer then peeks a second time. The dealer, in taking a second look, is uncertain whether or not the hole card is an ace. If the dealer turns over the ace, the hand is over anyway, but what happens if play resumes without the Blackjack? You can safely assume that the dealer has a low card in the hole—probably a four. The four looks like an ace and has momentarily confused the dealer. Orientals, who love to "squeeze" their two cards, call this a "Japanese Blackjack." If you put a face card on top of a four and squeeze the two cards, barely seeing the upper left-hand corner of the bottom card, you'll know what they mean. The best way to exploit the Double Peek is to stand on all stiff hands and double down if your hand totals 10 or 11.

Once you have successfully used the Double Peek you will be encouraged to look for other dealer tells. If you think you have discovered a dealer tell, you should be able to predict whether or not the dealer is stiff or pat at least 8 times out of 10. Do not play your hand any differently until you have achieved this 80% accuracy figure on at least 10 hands.

## BLACKJACK TIP #3: PLAYING "ON THE RUN" (FOR CARD COUNTERS ONLY)

Playing on the run is a lot of fun but you must be prepared to play short sessions in each casino; you must be prepared to take some heat; and you must limit your playing time on each casino shift.

To employ this technique you must learn to walk by a table, scan the cards and quickly pick up the count. If the running count is +6 or higher (in a six-deck game), sit down. You have an even game. Continue to play as long as the running count remains at +6 or above. Follow your money management formula for betting. When the count drops below +6 get up and leave the table. Continue walking and scanning for new opportunities. When the cut card comes out and the dealer prepares to shuffle, get up and leave. You don't want to waste your time waiting for a new shoe.

Yes, you can jump into any game anytime in the shoe. The cards in the discard tray that you haven't seen are considered as being behind the cut card. If you are an advanced player using the true count, your remaining decks start from the point at which you enter the game. For example, if you enter with three decks in the discard tray, and play through one deck, your remaining decks are now five for the play of the next hand (see next tip).

An example of "on the run" play occurred recently at the Resorts Casino in Atlantic City. A player entered the casino on a Tuesday evening about 10:30 p.m. He played about nine tables in five different pits. Many of the tables that he walked by yielded a count of +2 or +3. He paused and waited for the next hand to be dealt. If the count reached the +6 level he sat down. If it did not, he kept walking looking for another table. In one of the pits he took a lot of heat because he was betting from $5 to $500. He did not return to that pit.

He left Resorts at about 11:40 p.m. having won $850. You can use this technique to find a lot of high count tables but don't be tempted to sit down unless the running count is +6 (or +8 in an 8-deck game) or higher. If you play at anything less than +6, you are gambling and wasting your time. In general, the running count should equal the number of decks in the game before you sit down to play.

### BLACKJACK TIP #4: HOW TO HANDLE THE DISCARD TRAY WHEN PLAYING ON THE RUN (FOR CARD COUNTERS ONLY)

Playing on the run has become the accepted method of play for many of our BLACKJACK CLINIC graduates with whom we have kept in touch. If you take this approach, don't stand behind any one table too long because the floor persons and pit bosses have learned to recognize card counters that use this technique. My approach has been to perfect the "card counter's stroll." I stroll up and down the aisles glancing at each table as I walk around looking for a count of at least +6. If I get to +6, I hurriedly sit down to play the next hand. (If you are ever chatting with me inside a casino and all of a sudden I'm not there, you'll know what happened. I've developed a sixth sense about spotting these +6's. Sometimes it even takes me about an hour or more to get out of the casino after cashing in because I keep finding the +6's on the way out. One time, my wife, Nancy, was out the back door of Resorts walking toward the parking lot before she realized I was not there. She had to come back in to find me at a +6 table.)

Anyway, the question that most students ask is what about the discard tray? Doesn't this affect the +6 that you're getting? How do you handle the cards already in the discard tray? Should you only use this technique at the top of the shoe when you can keep track of the Zones? What if the discard tray already contains all of the high cards that the card counter is hoping will be left in the shoe?

The mathematically correct way to handle the discard tray when playing on the run is to mentally place all of the cards in the discard tray behind the cut card. You haven't seen the cards. You don't know what is behind the cut card. It's the same as starting with a new shoe except that your cut card is, of course, placed farther toward the front of the shoe. That is why it is safer, but not mandatory, to use this technique near the top of the shoe. If you jump in at the middle of the shoe, you are essentially playing in a game with a four- or five-deck cut card. This cuts down on your overall advantage *FOR THAT SHOE,* but still enhances your overall game and your profits. Remember, the trick is to assume that all the discards are behind the cut card and you're starting at base zero. Remember where you are in the discard tray.

## BLACKJACK TIP #5: PARLAY BETTING

Parlay Betting is necessary to protect placement of your cut card. If the casino floor person or pit boss believes you are sitting at a Blackjack table and counting, he may order the dealer to move the cut card forward in the deck, thereby reducing your advantage. To minimize the chance of this happening, you must appear to be betting as an average gambler. You must increase your bet only when you win. What this means is that you increase your bet only from money in the circle in front of you. You never increase your bet from money in your stack of chips in front of you. If you lose and the count goes up and indicates a higher bet, you ignore the higher bet and bet the same amount as you bet on the last hand.

Let's assume that you are betting $10 and the count shoots up and justifies a bet of $25. You win the hand. Twenty dollars is there sitting in the betting circle in front of you after the dealer pays your win. Your bet is $20 for the next hand. You have parlayed your bet. If you had lost this hand, you would then ignore the $25 bet and place another $10 bet.

One professional Blackjack player I know has been using this technique for years in Las Vegas and is doing very well with it.

His cover is excellent, and he has never had a cut card moved forward on him in any of the shoe games in Vegas. I highly recommend that you incorporate this betting technique into your playing procedures.

### BLACKJACK TIP #6: HOW TO GET AN 80 TO 1 BETTING SPREAD IN ATLANTIC CITY

It is possible to get as much as 80 to 1 betting spread in Atlantic City, but I don't recommend it unless you have a bankroll to finance such a spread, since you are not playing that many hours in any one casino and you are willing to "hit and run." In order to accomplish this you must do two things: You must give the appearance of being a gambler as your bet is progressing in size, and you must take the money and run when the cut card comes out. If your bet is progressing and you have lost two or three hands in a row, it is easy to exude the characteristics of a gambler by reaching into your pocket for your bankroll and coming out with the higher bets in an attempt to recoup. If you are winning you have to give the appearance of letting it ride. Going for the big kill—"one more time."

You are going to draw some heat with this approach so you have to schedule your playing time very carefully for each casino shift. At the conclusion of a big betting shoe the best approach is to leave the casino immediately after changing color and cashing out. The casino floor persons desire to minimize the number of fills for each of their Blackjack tables so their intent in asking to buy back your red or green chips is to reduce the possibility of having to request another fill. Sure they see how much you've won but so what. Just remember to reduce your exposure for that particular shift after a big win.

### BLACKJACK TIP #7: HOW TO IMPROVE YOUR PLAYING CONDITIONS IN THE NEVADA CASINOS

On your next weekend Blackjack trip, would you like to avoid the casino crowds and play hours of uninterrupted Blackjack?

Imagine three or four 45-minute sessions of a favorable two-deck game with one other player and the dealer. Enhance this enviable situation with a comfortable 8 to 1 spread, and you're outlining a profitable trip to your favorite gaming locale.

Using the following strategy, you can increase your playing time 30% in a typical trip. Equally important, you will have better conditions in which to play, fewer players per game, more ease to walk from a negative game, and more hands per hour in favorable conditions.

Count systems offer a range of advantages of 0 to 2%. This is at best a small advantage. To maximize your advantage you must "grind out" the casino—a reversal of the strategy the casinos use against unskilled players. However, "grinding" requires marathon sessions which are beyond the mental stamina of most weekend players. Logically your goal should be to improve your playing conditions. You can do this by playing the "off" hours.

Simply stated the strategy is: "Play when most people don't. Don't play when most people do." Basically, you want to play from 4:00 to 10:00 a.m.; 4:30 to 6:30 p.m.; and 8:00 to 10:00 p.m. As an example, think of your next 3-day, 2-night weekend trip to Las Vegas. Like most, you will arrive after 10:00 p.m. Instead of playing in your excited-but-tired condition, check in, set the alarm for 3:30 a.m. and go to sleep.

When you awake you will be rested and alert. However don't tip your hand to the casino personnel by bounding through their doors clean shaven and fresh pressed. You might as well wear a large red "C" on your chest. Put on the clothes from the night before. Don't brush out your hair too well, and where applicable, don't shave. You want that rumpled, been-up-all night look. It will disarm most casino people. Play at easy-to-find, uncrowded low stakes tables until mid to late morning. When the tourists and gamblers begin to fill the casinos, take a long break.

Mid-day is a good time for brunch and a review of the morning session. I always carry a pocket-size notebook and make quick notes concerning the morning session during this break. Work off the brunch and any tensions with a set of tennis or a swim in the hotel pool. A nap will also help you stay fresh for the evening sessions.

About 4:00 in the afternoon, many of the tourists are leaving the casinos to take naps or get ready for dinner. This is the time for you to get back to the tables. Normally you'll be able to play with few distractions until the tourists come back into the casinos around 6:00 p.m. to go to a dinner show or a restaurant. Generally, player traffic is moderate during dinner show hours—8:00 p.m. to 10:00 p.m. which is a good opportunity for you to cram in a short session. However, after 10:00 p.m. everyone is at the tables—your signal to stop until early morning.

There is one important point to remember about playing during light player traffic times. The chance of being closely observed is greater with fewer players at the tables. Be aware of the pit bosses—what they do and say, but don't let it unnerve you. The simplest tactic to distract them is to keep pulling folding green out of your pocket while dragging chips from play. Remember this makes you look like a loser. Limit your sessions in a casino to 45 minutes. To play longer gives the pit bosses too much time to observe your play and determine if you're counting.

Following this plan will improve the conditions under which you play and probably increase your playing time. Remember to play in off hours and stay loose and relaxed. Always analyze your plan immediately at the end of each session and make notes. Be aware of but don't worry about pit bosses. Put these suggestions into practice and you will reap the rewards.

## SHUFFLE-TRACKING: AN EASY WAY TO START

This technique is very usable when you have either a high plus or high minus count at the end of the shoe when the shuffle card comes out. It will not work in an 8/4 game (8 decks, 4-deck cut). It will work in an 8/2 game, a 6/2 game or any game where two or less decks are cut off (although you must have a shuffle that is trackable).

In an 8/2 game, you will be cutting 4, 3, or 2 decks to the front (extra high cards) or to the back (extra low cards). Remember at the end of the shoe, that a high + equals extra high cards and a high − equals extra low cards.

Here is how to track the end clump:

| |
|---|
| 8 |
| 7 |
| 6 |
| 5 |
| 4 |
| 3 |
| 2 |
| 1 |

) extra high or low
) cards are here

8-deck stack
immediately
preceding shuffle

| |
|---|
| 6 |
| 5 |
| 4 |
| 3 |
| 2 |
| 1 |

| |
|---|
| 8 |
| 7 |

Dealer's first move.
Note position of
end-clump now.

| |
|---|
| 7 |
| 6 |
| 5 |
| 4 |
| 3 |
| 2 |
| 1 |

| 8 |
|---|

Dealer's first
move may only
involve one deck

| 4 | 6 |
|---|---|
| 3 | 5 |
| 2 | 8 |
| 1 | 7 |

Dealer's second move
to line up stacks
before the shuffle.
Two-deck first move.

| 4 | 7 |
|---|---|
| 3 | 6 |
| 2 | 5 |
| 1 | 8 |

Dealer's second move
after one-deck
first move.

| |
|---|
| 1 + 7 |
| 2 + 8 |
| 3 + 5 |
| 4 + 6 |

Shuffled decks after two-deck first move. Dealer shuffles one deck at a time together from each stack. Note end-clump at top of new shuffle. Insert cut card as deep as possible if end-clump contains extra high cards. Cut top four decks to rear (insert cut card in middle) if end-clump contains extra low cards.

| | |
|---|---|
| 1 + 8 | ** |
| 2 + 5 | |
| 3 + 6 | * |
| 4 + 7 | |

Shuffled decks after one-deck first move. Note end-clump split between top and bottom. Insert cut card at position * if end-clump contains extra high cards; at ** if end-clump contains extra low cards.

You can refine your tracking of the end-clump by marking the count at the end of deck one for a one-deck first move, or at the end of deck two for a 2-deck first move.

Let's take an example. Suppose the count at the end of deck two is -8. This means that there are eight extra high cards in these first two decks. Mark or remember this count by using a chip or some other technique.

Now suppose that the count jumps up to +7 when the cut card comes out. Your end-clump contains seven extra high cards. If you control the cut card, your first four decks contain about 15 extra high cards. I say about 15 because errors will creep in through the shuffling process.

If, on the other hand, your marked count for decks one and two is +20 and you end up with a count of +10, what do you have? Extra high cards or low cards in the top four decks of the new shuffle? You have 10 extra low cards; +20 means 20 extra low cards; +10 at the end means 10 extra high cards. The difference is 10. Play around with this a little, but get a handle on the arithmetic.

Do not be tempted to bet too much off the top when you have cut extra high cards to the top of the shoe until you are confident that your tracking works. You can test your tracking by noting the count at the end of the first four decks. If you predicted 15 extra high cards, your count should be close to -15.

# CHAPTER TEN

# CHEATING

## by STANLEY ROBERTS

Casinos will do anything they can to stop the system player. These activities are known as casino countermeasures and they can be either honest or dishonest. (Knowledge, observation, and individual disguise are the player's best counter-countermeasures.) In this chapter, we will discuss honest countermeasures and dishonest countermeasures as they relate to casinos, dealers and players. And, lastly, we will discuss how to avoid being cheated.

## CASINOS

The concept that there is such a thing as an "honest" countermeasure is hard to accept. If a game is open to the public and all are allowed to play by a stated set of rules, then we think that the house must accept all players, good and bad alike. But, apparently, casinos only want bad players from whom they can take money. Somehow what the casinos preach and what they practice just don't ring true. The casinos want the public to think that Blackjack is a game of chance. We know it is a game of skill.

In Nevada, the ultimate casino countermeasure is to bar a player from playing Blackjack in that club. If the casinos did this to everyone who won, or to too many good players, the suckers would soon realize that that is what they are, and the game of Blackjack and casino profits would quickly die.

A popular countermeasure is to "Break the Deck" or reshuffle the cards. This might be done whenever a large bet is made, or if the dealer has been counting. Breaking the deck too often slows down the game and the casino's rate of profit. It really doesn't pay to do it against small-time players, since the overwhelming percentage of players are losers, and the house may be cutting its profits by a larger figure than they save from stopping the occasional system player.

Some casinos believe that fast dealers will discourage system players. If a person is using a difficult system, that may be so. If the player is a novice or slow, he will be confused by a fast dealer. However, a fast dealer is a boon to the good system player because there is no dealer who can deal fast enough to stop the practiced pro. The faster the dealer, the greater the number of hands, and consequently, profit per hour. If the dealer is too fast for you, just take your time in playing your hand.

Changing the deck frequently is a legitimate countermeasure that makes it difficult for cheating players to mark the cards. Some people remark that the deck is "hot" or "cold." This is just a gambler's superstition.

Dishonest countermeasures (another word for this phrase is cheating) involves the use of devices and/or sleight-of-hand. The former is not likely to be found in the larger casinos, as its capture by the Gaming Control Board constitutes *prima facie* evidence of cheating and would surely involve a large fine or loss of license. Sleight-of-hand is far more difficult to prove. It is here and gone like a flash of light, and its existence is difficult to prove without a camera—and cameras are forbidden in the casino!

Another way the casino can cheat the player is by removing cards from or adding cards to the deck. By removing 10's and aces, or adding 5's, 6's, and other small cards, the deck can be made to yield a higher advantage for the dealer. This is also a dangerous move, since the deck could be seized by the Gaming Control Board as evidence.

In multiple-deck games where a shoe (dealing box) is used, it is possible to rig the shoe to facilitate dealing seconds. This, too, is a dangerous practice for the casino to engage in since it is clearly a deliberate attempt to cheat.

## DEALERS

A clever dealer can cheat by using sleight-of-hand plays on the unwary player or players. Harold Smith, Jr., in his book, *I Want to Quit Winners,* said, "We could cheat all the time and they (agents of the Gaming Control Board) would never know it. We're far more expert at this business than they are."

While the larger casinos do not sanction dealer cheating, a dealer might cheat to cover up the fact that he or she is dipping into the till. The larger casinos have too much at stake to authorize their dealers to cheat. They can make more money at the Blackjack tables by dealing a fair game and allowing the uninformed player to lose his bankroll.

Since we have covered the subject of cheating in depth in our other books ( *Winning Blackjack* and *The Beginner's Guide to Winning Blackjack)* we will just briefly describe here the different ways a dealer can cheat.

A clever dealer may have the ability to STACK THE DECK. In order to accomplish this feat, first the dealer has to stack the deck, then make a false shuffle and nullify the player's cut.

One popular form of deck-stacking is referred to as the HIGH-LOW STACK as illustrated in Drawing #1.

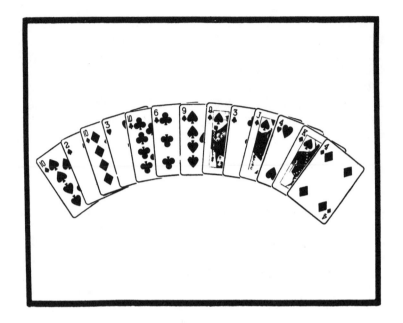

DRAWING #1

In this situation the order of cards is stacked so that every other card is high and the other is low. The power of this is twofold. If the dealer can arrange it, the player will get two low cards. If the dealer knows where the cards are, then he can deal seconds, as required, without having to peek at the top card.

Of course, the telltale giveaway in the deck-stacking game is the manner in which the cards are picked up. If you see any unusual arrangement of the discards by the dealer, watch out for a stacked deck. The dealer should pick up the cards one at a time from each hand. If he picks up several hands at once and appears to be rearranging the order, beware—grab your hat and leave.

Another form of stacking the deck is called the KENTUCKY STEP-UP, as illustrated in Drawing #2.

DRAWING #2

The cards are arranged as follows: 7,8,9,10,10,J,Q,K,A. If the cards are dealt from this stack to one player, the dealer will win the first two hands; to two players he will win the first round and have an ace for the second; to three players he will win the round from all.

Another little device is to get all of the 10's up front for the first few hands. By doing so, everyone will get a total of twenty, and push with the dealer. But the remainder of the hands will be played from a ten-poor deck.

In order for the stacking dealer to preserve his handiwork, he must execute a false shuffle. One procedure that is utilized is called the RIFFLESTACK. Although the deck is shuffled, a slug of cards which had been stacked is preserved and kept whole. This slug may be on the top, as illustrated in Drawing #3, or at the bottom, which makes it more difficult to detect.

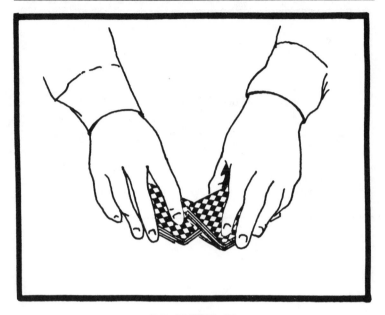

DRAWING #3

Another false shuffle is called the PULL THROUGH. The cards are shuffled in an angular manner; they are then pulled through each other. This sleight-of-hand as illustrated in Drawing #4 and #5, makes it appear as though the cards are being shuffled, but they are not.

DRAWING #4

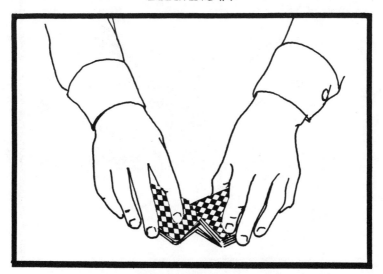

DRAWING #5

The principal way that cheating takes place at the Blackjack table is by the dealing of SECONDS, as illustrated in Drawing #6. A dealer who deals seconds simply takes the SECOND CARD from the deck instead of the first or top card. If you would like to know the value of this cheating play, deal a few hands as the dealer against an imaginary player. Whenever the top card is not suitable for your hand, take the next card. You will soon see how powerful having this choice is. In his new book, *The Mathematics of Gambling,* Thorp explains this in detail.

In order to utilize the technique of dealing the second card, first the dealer must know if the top card is one that he doesn't want, or if it is a beneficial card. He finds out by "peeking" at the top card. There are three basic kinds of peeks as illustrated in Drawings #7, #8, and #9.

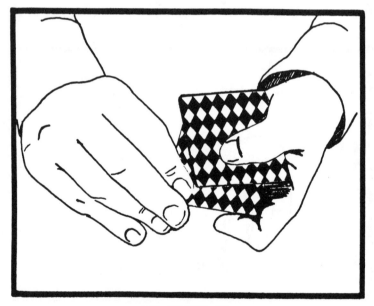

DRAWING #6

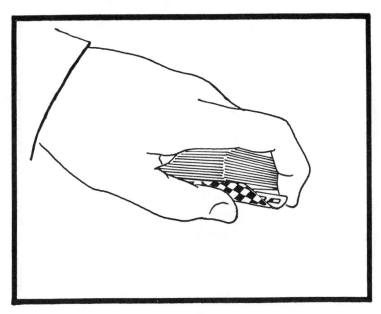

DRAWING #7

The FRONT PEEK is done with the dealer's palm downward and his hand toward the front. The top card is crimped so that a corner is visible. This is executed in such a manner that only the dealer can see the card.

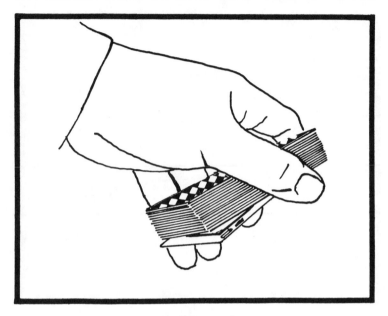

DRAWING #8

The BACK PEEK is done with the palm in a vertical position. The dealer's hand may be held in front, but it is usually held toward the side. The thumb is used to raise the card so that a corner is visible.

DRAWING #9

The TILT PEEK is performed by slipping the top card slightly forward and leaning it up by placing pressure on the front edge. If the deck is tilted forward, it is only necessary to tilt the top card slightly so that a corner is visible.

Some dealers use a "shiner" to peek at cards. This is a small reflective surface or mirror that is generally concealed at the edge of the table or is on top in a place like a pipe bowl. The top card is slid partially off the top of the deck and may be viewed in the reflected surface.

In this manner, the deck does not need to be turned over or sideways.

Another method of knowing the value of the top card is for the cards to be marked, which can be done in a number of ways. The cards can be marked with paint or daub; they can be scratched or bent; or they may actually be printed by a manufacturer of marked decks. The best way to detect a marked deck is to riffle the stack at rapid speed while keeping your eyes on one section of the pattern. If you note any variations, the deck is marked.

You will not ordinarily get the chance to riffle the deck in a casino; however, it is unlikely that a casino would use marked cards, because this constitutes *prima facie* evidence of cheating.

After the peeking dealer sees the top card, and he decides he does not want it, he must find some way of either getting rid of it or taking the next card, the SECOND CARD. One way to avoid the top card is to give it to a confederate who is sitting at third base. This confederate is usually referred to as an ANCHOR MAN. The dealer signals him to take the card or just deals it to him. If you observe the man at third base making unusual plays, it's time to leave. A second way to avoid taking the top card is to take the bottom card.

If a cheating dealer is a real craftsman, however, he is able to deal the second card without trouble and without detection. In order to deal the second card, the deck must be held in a particular way. This way is referred to as the MECHANIC'S GRIP, as illustrated in Drawing #10.

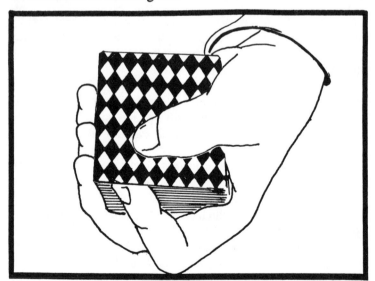

DRAWING #10

The corner of the deck is held between the index and middle fingers. The thumb is held in a more or less rigid position, which is usually referred to as the "dead thumb." When a dealer (non-cheating type) deals the cards, he pushes the top card forward with his thumb. The second-dealer must hold the top card in place rigidly with his thumb. A dealer who does not deal seconds will usually place all his fingers along the side of the deck, rather than placing his index finger in the front. When dealing seconds, the thumb is used to move the top card slightly, so that the edge of the second card is exposed. Then, by holding the top card firm, the second card is dealt. The finger is used to keep the third and fourth card in position. An expert moves the deck so slightly that only a professional can detect his moves.

## PLAYERS

Players who cheat are no threat to other players unless the cheating player is a confederate of the dealer. However, we would advise moving to another table since the more relaxed and worry-free you are, the better you can play regardless of the system you are using.

## HOW TO AVOID BEING CHEATED

There are a number of techniques which will assist you in avoiding cheaters. No system can win against a stacked deck or a mechanic. Therefore, you must avoid the cheating dealer to the best of your ability. You can do it by possessing knowledge of what to look for, being watchful of what the dealer is doing, discouraging the casino from cheating you (by not appearing to be a winner), and regularly moving (to limit the effect of any cheater on your bankroll).

One of the best ways to avoid being cheated is to look like a loser. The casino has nothing to fear from the average player, so it is normally satisfied to win from him at the typical rate of loss.

Concealing your winnings as described in depth in Chapter Fourteen is another way to avoid being cheated.

If the dealer does anything to make you feel suspicious—even though you cannot put your finger on it—assume he is doing something to your disadvantage. You should be particularly suspicious if there is more than one incident of a similar nature. If cards are incorrectly dealt and strange things seem to be happening with the hands, assume the worst—unless you know that the dealer's fumblings are due to the fact that he is a break-in or new dealer who has no card-handling experience. Be particularly wary of the "old man" who has apparent difficulty in dealing.

Perhaps the best way to avoid being cheated is to regularly move around. This will give you the added bonus of being less familiar to dealers and floormen. Never permit yourself to lose more than 10% of your bankroll at any one table. If and when this occurs, get up and leave. You may have been cheated.

Remember, you are safer in the larger casinos—they have more to lose if they are caught cheating and their eye-in-the-sky watches the dealers as well as the players.

# CHAPTER ELEVEN

# TEAM PLAY
# AND OTHER ADVANCED TECHNIQUES

## by KEN USTON

### THE BIG PLAYERS AND THE LITTLE COUNTERS

There is a rather ingenious approach to playing Blackjack that in effect allows the player to enjoy betting ratios of 1,000 to 1 or even greater. It is particularly effective in multiple-deck games. This method, known as *team play,* involves careful training, coordination and synchronized signaling between several players.

Each of several "counters" are stationed at four or five different tables in a four-deck club. The counters make minimum bets, usually flat betting, and play Basic Strategy. They count down the shoe, preferably all using the same counting system. When the deck becomes sufficiently "hot" (rich in high cards), the counter calls in the "Big Player" through some furtive signal. The Big Player then places a big bet at the counter's table, as he receives the "count" and the number of aces played from the counter through the use of a pre-determined set of signals.

The Big Player continues to play at the table until the shoe either runs out or is no longer favorable to the player. Then he leaves the table and waits to receive similar signals from other counters in the casino.

The net result of this approach is that the Big Player (henceforth referred to as the BP) NEVER plays in negative situations. He has an edge over the house on every bet. The counters, of course, are playing at a disadvantage to the house, approximately −.5%, but their small losses are offset many times over by the BP's wins.

I was first introduced to high-rolling through this approach. Our team, which eventually reached a total of over 20 members, consisted of three BP's and 17 counters. The large size was particularly effective because it allowed us to rotate counters between the clubs and shifts in such a way that the pit bosses infrequently saw the same counters and BP's together. The team won about $1,000,000 in Las Vegas and Europe before we were finally apprehended at the Sands. The method became widely known among pit personnel and our team disbanded. I wrote a book about the experience entitled, *The Big Player,* which, I am happy to relate, is being made into a major motion picture. The rights were bought by Frank Capra, Jr., and Dale Crase.

The team concept sounds simple—and it is. The recruitment, training, and scheduling problems involved in the team approach, however, are formidable indeed. Counters first had to be trained to count four-deck shoes accurately and rapidly. They then learned to convert the "running" count to a "true count," which is a more accurate way to measure player advantage. This is done by adjusting the number of aces played AND determining the number of decks remaining in the shoe. It took most counters from six to eight weeks of training to be ready for a "trip" with the team.

After learning how to count, the counter was trained in the proper ways of smoothly and subtly conveying the signals. We used two sets of signals to convey the count, a set of "arm" signals and a set of "chip" signals. The number of aces was conveyed by the placement of the right hand on various parts of the body.

The BP had to know far more about the game than the counters. After receiving the running count and the number of aces, the BP had to reflect the number of aces "rich" or "poor" in the running count and divide the number of half-decks remaining to be dealt, to derive the "adjusted true count." He would then compare this number to a predetermined betting formula to calculate the size of his bet.

When we first started, we would typically bet $500 (or $1,000 if allowed by the club maximum) at a true count of +6. Toward the end of the venture, when we were playing to banks of $150,000 and, once, of over $200,000, we would bet $2,000 at a true count of +3; $4,000 at a count of +5; and whatever we could get on the table (up to seven hands of $1,000) at true counts of +7 or greater.

The BP had to know the "numbers," a matrix of about 140 numbers reflecting the true count at which various plays would be made; that is, when deviations from Basic Strategy were required. For example, the "number" we used to split 10's against a dealer's 6 up-card was +5; i.e., if the true count equaled or exceeded +5, we would split; otherwise, we would stand.

The "team approach" was first employed, to my knowledge, in the late 1960's when a team from Texas was formed. Reliable firsthand sources indicate that the team won somewhere around $300,000 before its techniques were finally detected by an alert pit boss at the Tropicana. Their signals were somewhat obvious (for example, when a deck was "hot," the counter would stand up to signal the BP to join his table). The team was totally exposed when a suspicious pit boss followed the group out of the casino after the session and noticed them getting into four different cars—all with Texas license plates.

Our team began operations in 1974 and continued successfully for about two years. Pit bosses were generally confounded with the strange modus operandi of the BP, who would wander from table to table in a seeming erratic pattern, making bets in what seemed to be a totally random fashion. The team moved from club-to-club with our three BP's, and continually rotated counters to try to avoid pit bosses associating counters with BP's.

For a period of about three months, the three BP's (the other two were named Barry and Steve in *The Big Player)* were among the very highest rollers in Vegas. Most high rollers bet in increments of $100. Our mega-rollers never bet less than $500 per hand and often would have $7,000 on the table at one time. On many occasions, all three BP's were "comped" at various hotels, enjoying suites, gourmet restaurants, and, occasionally, when time allowed, the shows. On one trip, total BP comps totaled well over $5,000, as I was treated to lavish suites at the Sands, Barry enjoyed the hospitality of Caesars Palace, and Steve was comped at the MGM.

But it seems that all good things come to an end. An alert boss at the Sands noticed that whenever I approached a table, someone at the table was always scratching his arm or body in other than a completely normal fashion. He apparently put his "eye-in-the-sky" to work on his suspicions, and after several weekends of play, I was finally detained in a backroom, questioned by the police, and "86'd" from the hotel. One of our counters was arrested, although the judge later dismissed the charges. I initiated legal action against the hotel, the first of several lawsuits pertaining to my being barred that I would be filing.

About a year later, I formed a team that used the same approach and had success for a period of about nine months.

Our betting levels were lower, but I (sometimes in disguise) and three other BP's once again began extracting fairly significant sums from the casinos. Other barrings followed—at the Fremont, Dunes, Hilton, MGM, Marina, and the Sands. But, as Joe Namath once said, "Nothing hurts when you win."

## UNFAIR PLAYER ADVANTAGES

A common complaint of many pit bosses is that card counters invariably progress into more *gamey* aspects of the game, as they become enamored with the general concept of supporting themselves on revenues extracted from casinos. There are degrees of *gaminess* in these techniques, some of which are legal, and some of which are clearly illegal and in fact constitute a felony.

I must hasten to add that although I am familiar with these techniques, it is not because I participated in them.

I am often approached by counters and others aware of my experience in counting who make various proposals to me. Further, several ex-teammates, converting to some of these techniques, have related their experiences to me.

I would also emphasize to those players that I had refrained from writing about front-loading and spooking for many years. I discuss them now only because they have already been documented in print.

## FRONT-LOADING

Probably the most profitable, and paradoxically also the most innocuous of the *hole-card* techniques, "front-loading," refers to the practice of observing the dealer's hole card as it is dealt. A dealer of a hand-held single or double-deck game will occasionally expose his hole card as he sweeps the card under his up-card. If the card is visible on each round, the dealer is referred to as a "100% loader." The player who knows how to capitalize on the added knowledge of the dealer's hole card can increase his edge over the house by as much as 5% or more.

Previous texts have stated that knowledge of the hole card adds nearly 10% to the player's theoretical edge. The practical advantage is far less since there are many plays which can never be made; they would expose the technique. For example, knowing the dealer has a 19, it would be tempting, but also foolish, to hit a hard 18. The power of front-loading is demonstrated when one considers that perfect knowledge of the insurance bet alone adds over 2% to the player's edge!

Novice dealers are more likely to expose their hole card when dealing. The card is often observed from third base, as the right-handed dealer sweeps the card under his up-card, after having dealt to the position at third base. Other dealers are observable from the fourth or fifth spot on the table. Others tilt the deck such that the card is observed from the middle of the table, or even from the second spot.

I personally feel that playing a front-loader is not only legal, but constitutes a totally legitimate pursuit. As one Nevada judge once said when a casino detained a player for "peeking" at the hole card, "If the house is going to show the card, there's no reason why the player can't look."

I recall one dealer, a middle-aged blonde named Sylvia, in a Reno Club, who had a lot of "juice" in her casino. Sylvia showed her hole card with amazing regularity; it was observable from the middle of the table.

Card counters and other teams pounded her mercilessly week after week. But because she was a friend of the Shift Manager and in fact had taken trips in the owner's private jet, the bosses let her continue dealing Blackjack despite these losses, since she was totally above suspicion of cheating and one of the club's most experienced dealers. Still, Sylvia's losses continued heavily and relentlessly. One day a teammate entered the club and was dismayed to find she had been (permanently) relegated to dealing roulette!

## SPOOKING

Spooking is the technique of reading a dealer's hole card from the rear of the table when the dealer checks for Blackjack. Thus, the hole card is readable only when the dealer has a ten or an ace up-card about 38% of the time. The player behind the dealer, the "spook," conveys to the player at the table through signaling whether the dealer is "stiff" (i.e., has a poor hand) or "pat" (has a good hand). The player adjusts his playing strategy accordingly.

I believe spooking constitutes an unfair player edge over the house. In my opinion it is not dissimilar to stationing an agent behind a poker player to signal the value(s) of the player's hole cards, a practice which is clearly considered cheating at poker.

The player edge is increased from spooking by approximately 2%. This again is not as great as the theoretical edge because of certain plays that cannot be made for cover purposes. The technique allows even the non-counting player to enjoy a modest edge over the house.

Teams of players have attempted to convey the value of the dealer's hole card through mechanical signaling devices, clearly a risky practice since the players, if caught, carry physical evidence of their activity. On one occasion in downtown Las Vegas, a player in a wheelchair was receiving signals from a "spook" who was playing at a table to the rear of his dealer. The "spook" was apprehended and detained. The other player jumped out of his rented wheelchair and ran out the door of the casino—alas, to no avail—he was captured and arrested several hundred yards down Virginia Street.

The most amazing "spooking" opportunity I have ever seen existed in El Casino in Freeport several years ago. The dealers there, incredibly, were instructed not to bend the cards when checking for Blackjack. As a result, they exposed the *entire* hole card during the process of looking at their bottom card. It was quite tempting to want to station a spook to the rear of the dealer. I personally know several groups that resorted to this technique in El Casino.

Spooking is not possible in Atlantic City, where the dealer doesn't look at his hole card until after the players have played their hands. It's obviously not possible in casinos where the dealer does not take a hole card, such as in France, England and some casinos in the Caribbean.

## PLAYING WITH THE HELP

This practice, a felony, requires collusion between the dealer and a player. The dealer, after checking for Blackjack, will signal the player whether he is "pat" or "stiff." The player adjusts his playing strategy accordingly, securing an additional edge over the house of approximately 2%.

The typical financial arrangement has been for the dealer to share in one-third of the win, and to agree to "make-up time" with the player if a loss is experienced until the duo gets into the winning column. This practice can also lead to the dealer cheating other players, if he's capable, to insure that his overall win-loss rate is not out-of-line with other dealers.

Clever signaling is virtually undetectable either from the pit or from the "sky." For example, the dealer could blink for "pat" hands and not blink for "stiff" hands; or point at the first-base player prior to that player playing his hand if he has a "pat," and not point if he has a stiff. He might move back almost imperceptibly from the table if "pat," and so on. Signals can be made even more subtle by using one signal if the up-card (ten or ace) is red, a second signal if it is black. There are so many signaling alternatives that it is virtually impossible to "pick off" this play by spotting the signals.

I have been approached on numerous occasions by dealers and others with offers to "play with the help." I am continually amazed at the number of people who are willing to risk a felony conviction to win money at the Blackjack tables. Perhaps this is one reason the bosses remain suspicious of all players so continually. I have never "played with the help" and strongly advise against it.

A more subtle form of "playing with the help" occurs continually probably in every casino with hand-held decks in Nevada. It is also nearly impossible to prevent. With a ten or ace up, the dealer knows whether he is pat or stiff. Thus he is able to determine if a player should hit or stand on his hand. On literally countless occasions, a male dealer, to curry favor with a female player, will pass the girl by if he has a "stiff" or pause, a non-verbal hint that a hit is in order, if he is "pat." My sister, a non-counter, but an attractive girl, tells me that more often than not, a male dealer will accord her this "courtesy." Even though she plays an atrocious game of Blackjack (at $5 per hand), I wouldn't be surprised if she has a slight overall edge over the house. Many dealers extend this courtesy to family, friends, and others and a surprising number of them will brag about their willingness to do so at the least expression of interest. One reason why so many houses forbid dealers from playing at the club where they work is to avoid undue "chumminess" between the dealer and the players.

## MUCKING

"Card mucking" is a highly effective way of securing an edge over the house of 20% or greater. It requires great skill and a larcenous heart. The player, after hitting a hand several times, using legerdemain, will retain one of the cards. He will substitute that card as appropriate to improve subsequent hands. To demonstrate how powerful this technique is, let me give you an example:

A player has a two-card total of seven and hits his hand with several low cards, perhaps three or four, purposely "breaking" (going over twenty-one). As he throws his hand in, he keeps a five. His next hand is a ten, six. He hits, draws a ten and substitutes the five for one of the tens in his hand, giving him a total of "21." His next hand is an ace, four. He substitutes the ten for the four, and turns over his Blackjack. The process goes on and on. The player, flat betting $500 or $1,000, can make a quick score of thousands of dollars and be out the door of the club before the pit knows what hit them.

Clubs which deal multiple-deck games face down are particularly subject to the ravages of card muckers. Since it is impractical to change decks frequently or to quickly ascertain whether or not all the cards are in the deck, this is why most multiple-deck games are dealt face up. It is also why, in the single-deck clubs, the decks are often changed quite abruptly—immediately after which the boss checks the deck to ensure that it is a complete one.

Needless to say, I have never been involved in any way in any such operation; however, I have observed muckers in action. There are revealing moves which can be spotted by the experienced observer which tend to give the mucker away. Yet, the competent mucker, like the experienced cheating dealer, is so smooth and his movements so quick and subtle that it's virtually impossible to detect mucking. As in any other profession, legal or otherwise, extensive training and prior preparation are necessary to increase the likelihood of success. Some muckers employ mechanical devices, called "holdouts," usually hidden under the right sleeve, which can exchange cards. These devices often work quietly, quickly and subtly. They are risky, however, since they constitute prima facie evidence of cheating.

## CARD MARKING

A common form of player cheating is to mark, bend, or wave cards of certain value. In hand-held games, particularly, the player is then able to determine the value of either the dealer's hole card, the next card to be dealt, or both. The pit can guard against this by checking the deck after play for unusual marks, waves, ripples or other evidence of the deck being tampered with. But as in anything else, the accomplished bender can usually fool even the most experienced of bosses.

## CAPPING

"Capping" (or "pressing") involves the player increasing the size of his bet *after* he has been dealt a good hand (or decreasing it after he's been dealt a poor hand). While there are frequent attempts by amateurs to cap bets, the highly trained, experienced "capper" is difficult to spot, either from the pit or from the "sky." One "capper" at a large club in Reno was so smooth and his movements so subtle, that the bosses let him play for over an hour, as they filmed him from the "sky." The film is now used in the club's pit boss orientation.

"Cappers" can work in teams. When they do, the confederates usually sit at opposite ends of the table. For example, the player at third base might have a $200 bet out. Just as he's dealt a Blackjack, the player at first base spills his drink. The dealer is distracted and reaches out to protect the cards on the table from the drink. By the time she gets to third base, the player with the Blackjack has a $500 bet out. The dealer, though instructed to try to remember what each player has bet, isn't sure in all the commotion of the amount of the original bet. Our third baseman just made a $450 profit. He can make a nice living doing this just once a day.

Capping is particularly frowned upon in Atlantic City and I would caution anyone from even attempting it there. Not too long ago, one of the counters enjoying the game at Resorts International had a $500 bet out in the form of one purple chip. He'd been playing for ten hours and was fatigued. He won the hand and, concentrating on calculating the size of his next bet, inadvertently drew back his $500 bet and placed $1,000 (two purple chips) on the betting circle. The dealer, unaware of the change, paid the player $1,000 for the winning hand. The player, sensing an opportunity for a quick $500 profit, withdrew all four chips. Alas, the cameras in the sky and the bosses in the pit both picked up this action. The player was arrested, brought to jail, and his bankroll of about $5,000 was taken from him. He was released ten hours later on $5,000 bail and was told that the State was going to try to incarcerate him for from five to ten years!

The point here is that the New Jersey authorities are out to make examples of casino cheats to let the public know, quickly and early, that cheating will not be tolerated in New Jersey. Let the cheater beware!

## THE PERFECT PLAYER

Academicians love to argue incessantly on the question of what system is the most accurate. Paper after paper is presented at the Annual Gaming Conference each year, citing the value of the seven in betting, the player gain from a multi-parameter count, ad infinitum. These are interesting mathematical problems, and I'm glad that there are theoreticians who are concerned with solving these academic perplexities.

However, it is more important to the professional player to recognize that most responsible systems are capable of winning at close to the same rate. It is far more important to play responsible winning systems well then to be concerned with whether a system will yield an additional .01% over some less powerful system.

The main point is: There was a period in early 1977 when my Team #3 played with the most powerful system available. And most of my players didn't even know how to count!!

How was this possible? We used a portable micro-computer, capable of playing perfect Blackjack beyond the ability of the human brain. The computer was an ingenious device, developed partially through the financing of Team #2, by an electronics wizard from the Bay Area.

The "input" device consisted of four buttons which were programmed to accept "binary" information. That is, the first button represented the value "1," the second, "2," the third, "4," and the fourth, "8." Any number from one through 16 could be inputted by pushing the correct combination of buttons.

The computer itself (or "CPU" as the scientists call it) was about as long and wide as a pack of cigarettes and half as thick. The smallness was made possible through recent advances in the manufacturing of micro-processors and other miniature electronic components.

The output device was a small "tapper" (housed in an empty rouge case!) which buzzed with little signals designating both numerical information and hitting, standing, and other codes. Finally, attached to the computer, was a battery pack, two groups of four conventional batteries that powered the computer for about 4 to 6 hours before they had to be changed.

I practiced with the inventor for about two weeks. February 1, 1977, was the historic date on which a player first utilized a totally practical, portable micro-computer in a casino. I bet from one to four nickel chips ($5) at the Golden Gate casino in downtown Las Vegas and won $190. One of my teammates observed me, using a conventional count as I played the computer "count." He later stated that the differences in betting and playing strategy were frequent.

For the next 25 days I utilized the computer (we called it "George") and won $23,000 for the team. I won at a rate of about 2%, with a one-to-four betting ratio. On February 2, I graduated to quarters and soon was betting one-to-four black ($100) chips. My organizational bent led me to form a team, Team #3, to more fully capitalize on this technological golden goose. Within several weeks, four more counters were trained to operate "George." Murphy's law applied in spades as we were continually faced with the need to solder broken connections, replace discharged batteries, fixing loose switches and solving a myriad of technological problems. Our learning experience was so painful that the first bank, including my $23,000 win, resulted in a loss of over $20,000. The players were making errors; "George" still had "bugs" and would occasionally tilt. The team became discouraged and we took a break. I went to Europe for a few weeks where, using my brain for a change, I won about $5,000 in London and Loews' Monte Carlo.

When I returned from Europe, we once again attacked the electronics problem, this time with the experience of having solved the many bugs, problems and human errors so prevalent in the previous effort. The team grew to 16 people and we attacked the graveyard shift in Las Vegas, winning over $100,000 in two weeks of play. We were getting heat all over town—from the Griffin agents, the Gaming Commission, and dozens of pit bosses, who wondered why these players who were hitting 17's, doubling on 12, and splitting 6's versus an ace kept winning.

To alleviate the "heat," we decided to go to Tahoe. We won $24,000 on our first night. The second day, always "going for the gusto," I dispatched four players. We had one player in Harrah's, betting from one hand of $100 to two hands of $1,000. There were two players at the Sahara Tahoe doing the same thing. We felt our one player in Harvey's was almost wasting time, betting only to two hands of their lower limit, $500.

Apparently The Lake couldn't take that much action at one time. Gaming Control agents were summoned apparently after the previous night, when our four people had pounded the casinos so heavily.

One of our players was brought into the back room of Harrah's and searched. At first, they probably suspected he was equipped with some sort of electronic bomb. Our man hastily explained that it was only a computer. The Gaming Control agents ran over to Harvey's and detained two teammates there as well. The rest of our group sensed the heat and managed to avoid detention. But the three teammates who were caught, were arrested, charged with "bunko-Steering" and released on $2,000 bail each. They were not arraigned.

After nearly three weeks, we were finally able to get the D.A. to tell us that he would not arraign our people until the FBI had determined whether our little devices were, in fact, cheating devices. So, "George" went to Washington. It took the FBI five months to report back to the Commission that, in their opinion, the computers did not constitute cheating devices. The charges were dismissed and our bail (but not our "Georges") was returned.

In the interim, we decided to try to develop an improved "George" totally contained in a pair of shoes. The electronics and technology were there; the human ability was not. After losing $50,000, of which over $20,000 was in expenses (including a not insignificant bill from the shoe man), the project was abandoned. It seemed a binary toe input was beyond the ability of most of our people, who placed over $16,000,000 in action and sustained a $30,000 playing loss. There are several coordinated people who were able to make the "shoe George" work; but unfortunately, most of our people could not. I left electronics and returned to the world of cerebral Blackjack.

As computer technology increases, so does the casino's ability to detect such instruments. Conversely, a good counter also has to take countermeasures (such as disguises, low profile casino deportment, etc.). But, after all, the name of the game is Blackjack, and it's excitement all the way!

# CHAPTER TWELVE

# GETTING BARRED

## by KEN USTON

One of the primary occupational hazards of playing Blackjack is being forbidden from playing. The right to bar players is assumed by most casinos in Nevada, by those in England, and by casinos in Panama. It is not permitted in New Jersey.

The serious Blackjack player, whether he be a full-time professional or an avocational weekend player, must be knowledgeable in the techniques of barring, understand how to avoid being barred, and apply the proper methods of conduct if he happens to get barred.

## HOW IT HAPPENS

Casinos justifiably have the right to throw out or detain players who are cheating at the tables. These cheats would include practitioners of some of the techniques discussed in the previous chapter, including mucking, capping, and card marking. However, casinos also, I feel unjustifiably, assume the right to throw out skillful players as well; ones they consider to be sufficiently skillful at counting cards such that they have turned the odds in their favor.

Once the bosses have determined that a player is skilled, they will resort to various techniques. Rather than attempting to generalize the behavior of a wide variety of people, I will instead cite examples of the types of barrings that have actually occurred that involved me, my teammates, and others with whom I have discussed this issue.

The most typical form of barring is for the pit boss to come to the player's table and inform him that he is not welcome to play. This conversation usually sounds something like this:

"Okay, buddy. We don't want your action here. Hit the front door."

"You've just made your last bet," pushing the player's chips back from the betting square.

To the dealer, "Deal him out," without a word to the player.

On occasion, the techniques can get more stringent. My very first barring was at the Sands Hotel several years ago. As I was requesting $5,000 in markers at a table, the floorman said, "We've got a problem. Come to the cage."

At the cage, the Shift Manager asked me to step into the back office. I happily obliged, not suspecting at the time that anything was wrong. In the back office was a plainclothes policeman, who asked me questions about my address and occupation. He said, "You can consider yourself under arrest."

The Shift Manager ordered my picture taken with a polaroid camera and had me frisked. I was then read the "Trespass Act," which effectively said that if I returned to the Sands or any other Hughes Hotel, I would be subject to arrest.

I returned to my suite, packed my bag, took $45,000 in cash out of the casino cage and my safe deposit box, and took a cab to the Dunes. Four hours later, not having turned a single card, I was asked to leave the Dunes. The Dunes barring went like this:

Two security guards spotted me sitting in the cocktail lounge with three friends.

"Mr. Uston?"

"Yes?"

"Come with us."

I left the lounge, and they told me to follow them. We took an elevator to my room; my key didn't work since the lock had been adjusted. Inside the room, one of the guards read me the Trespass Act as I packed my bags.

The guards escorted me to the cage, where I was given my $45,000, neatly pre-packaged, and I was led out to the front door. On the way out, I asked the guards, "Why do I have to leave?"

One guard said, "I don't know. The manager who ordered this went home at midnight. They never tell us nuthin' here."

I filed two lawsuits three weeks later.

My most unpleasant barring occurred at the Mapes Moneytree in Reno in August, 1978. I'd been playing at the Mapes in my "cowboy" disguise ("Howdy, I'm Billy Williams. Mah friends call me Tex!"). I'd deposited $7,000 in the Mapes' cage and had been playing there for four days. I'd won a few thousand dollars, and most of the pit seemed quite cordial to me.

On the fourth night, I was comped at Mr. M's (a flambe-type gourmet restaurant on the mezzanine level of the Moneytree). While waiting for my table, I went down to the casino. I played a few hands. The pit was so cordial they raised the limit from $300 to $500 for me. As part of my cover, I ordered a bottle of Gevray Chambertin wine from the restaurant.

A formally attired headwaiter descended the escalator with a bucket and a towel over his arm. He uncorked the bottle at my table and handed me the cork. I sniffed it, approved, and also approved the taste that he poured into my wine glass. I tipped the waiter seven dollars, as he left the bottle of wine on my table. It seemed as though they liked my action.

During the play, the bosses were apparently completely bamboozled. I was varying my bet from one hand of $25 to two hands of $500, and they loved it. The pit personnel changed. It was my last day in Reno, so I violated a cardinal rule, DO NOT PLAY THROUGH A SHIFT CHANGE.

I detected a chill in the pit. Someone in the new shift apparently recognized me. After a while, I was asked to leave. I was incredulous, as I was escorted out the door of the casino. My friend had been eating at Mr. M's. I decided to inform him that I'd be waiting at the Sahara. I went back up to the restaurant, taking the SIDE door so that I wouldn't have to go through the casino.

At the top of the escalator, I was met by the tall unfriendly Shift Manager, who grabbed my jacket by the collar and pushed me onto the down stairs of the escalator. At the bottom, we were joined by a large plainclothes security guard who was told to, "Get rid of this f__ing punk."

I was herded out the door and in the alley was called a "f__ing punk" about five or six times.

I tried in vain to explain to the manager and the guard that I was merely trying to play Blackjack, that I was an invited "comped" guest at the Mapes and so on. This was to no avail. The epithets continued. Finally, I realized my urging was fruitless, and I turned to leave, saying, "Well, then you're a f__ing punk, too."

That was a mistake. The next thing I knew I was on the ground. I reached up and felt a sickening crinkling around my left eye. The net result was that the guard, a former Coast Guard boxer, had shattered my left cheek bone which required plastic surgery seven days later. Not a pleasant experience.

On January 1979, my Team #5 and I were playing at Resorts International in Atlantic City. We had been playing there for about nine days and we had $145,000 of the casino's money. We'd heard through the grapevine that barring was imminent, and we managed to get all our players out of the casino.

But, we had $43,000 in chips. Since I felt I'd be the one most likely not to be allowed to play in the future, I was elected to carry the chips to the cashier's cage.

At the cage, an entourage of security guards and compliance officers approached me. One compliance officer asked my name, address, phone number and social security number. He read to me from a little card.

"You are considered to be a professional card counter and you are not allowed to gamble at any Blackjack table in this casino. If you do so, you will be evicted for being a disorderly person. If you then return, I will have you arrested for trespassing."

I said, "Yessir," took my $43,000 and split.

Other barrings can be far more mellow. One of my teammates was once told, "Listen, Steve, please don't play on my shift. What you do on the other shifts here is not my business though."

The MGM's Vic Wakeman once told me, "Kenny, you're just too tough for us. Feel free to play baccarat or anything else, but, please, not Blackjack."

Flattery such as this makes it easier for the counter to accept a barring.

The mildest barring I know of came at the Marina, when the Casino Manager came up and said, "Kenny, I've got an idea. Rather than playing, why don't you and your girlfriend have dinner on us at our new gourmet restaurant."

The dinner was delicious.

So barring techniques vary widely, from getting comped to a lavish dinner, to getting put in the hospital with a shattered cheekbone. The good counter recognizes that training, practicing, and playing the game accurately are merely components of being successful at Blackjack. As in any other profession, he must also know how to avoid losing his job which, in this case, means how to avoid getting barred.

## HOW TO AVOID GETTING BARRED

The counter should try to put himself in the shoes of the typical floorman. Floormen welcome high-rolling losers, tourists who come to the casino to have a good time. The typical loser dresses flashily and tosses money around in the hedonistic casino environment as if it's not important to him. After all, he's there to have fun. Chances are he's loud, boisterous, has a good-looking girl hanging on his arm and drinks a lot.

The counter, on the other hand, will tend to be studious,

resembling a college professor or graduate student. He probably is quiet, since he has to concentrate on the count. He doesn't drink, watches all the cards on the table (maybe even moves his lips), and carefully places his bets on the table in accordance with his calculations. He probably doesn't get too upset when he loses if he's a good counter, because he knows that he will win in the long run.

The counter must come across as the tourist. It's not that difficult if he's a good actor. (It's for that reason that I got away with one hand of $25 to two hands of $500 at the Mapes.)

It's not possible to codify the optimum way for a counter to act in a casino; there are too many variables, such as the method of behavior in which the counter feels most comfortable, and the stereotypes and prejudices of the particular bosses against whom he is playing. So, I'll just include some tips—some of the things I do. Although I get barred many times, it's almost always because I'm recognized, rather than due to my casino comportment. Believe me, these techniques really work.

Often when starting a session, I'll go to the bar and order a scotch and water and a tall glass of water. I drink the water and pour the scotch and water (but not the ice) into the large water glass. Then I keep the scotch glass, full of ice and sort of "stagger" to the tables.

After a few bets, I'll loudly ask for "cocktails." When the waitress comes to take my order, if the pit boss is listening, I'll be sure to order a "double," in a loud voice.

The double sits on the table until a convenient negative deck comes along. Then it's to the men's room and the double scotch becomes a glass of water. Back to the table I go, chug-a-lugging the water.

Bosses obviously are quite interested in the betting levels of suspected counters. Cover betting strategy is an important aspect of fooling the bosses. Many counters bet one unit off the top and raise their bets only if the count increases. Others start at two units, go down if the deck gets negative and up if it becomes positive. These are good ways to get barred.

The player should bet in an apparently erratic pattern.

His off-the-top bet should appear to be a function of his idio-syncracies, rather than the fact that the deck has just been shuffled. Let's say you're playing to a moderate bankroll, trying to get variation from $25 to $300.

Generally, off the top, bet $75 to $100. In a single-deck Strip game, the player is dead-even with the house and can bet more than a minimum bet without unduly risking his bankroll. But mix it up. Bet one hand of $25 and one of $50. Bet three hands of $25. Bet one hand of three green chips, one red one, and two silvers. The dealers and bosses will be so busy concentrating on the pay-off if you get a Blackjack (or Surrender), that they'll not be worrying about the total amount of your bet.

If the count goes up, it's all right to parlay like most of the books tell you. But do it recklessly, as if you were a tourist. Don't carefully count out the number of chips. If you have a 3% edge, it's not that important whether you happen to throw out $215 or $275.

Mixing colors is effective. Three green chips and one black one to the pit looks like a small stack of green and black chips. One green chip and three blacks is a stack of the same size, but worth nearly twice as much. Betting this way makes it difficult for the boss to calculate your winnings.

Bet one green chip on one square and one black chip on another square off the top. If the count goes up, consolidate to three blacks and a green on one circle. If it goes down, drop to two greens and a red on one circle and one green on another circle. The bosses will think you're superstitious with your weird color-varying style. More importantly, they probably won't take the time to figure out the exact amount of each bet. They'll be concentrating on pay-outs.

Compare this to the player who methodically bets two green off the top and goes to either one green in negative decks or four green in positive decks. Not only does he get MORE heat, he gets LESS bet variation.

The "steaming" approach is one that works for me. I've gotten 30-to-1 or 40-to-1 ratios with it. To best describe it, I'll give an example of an almost unbelievable experience I had. Hard to believe, but it really happened.

I walked into the Hilton and cashed in three $100 bills for green ($25) chips. In order not to excite the bosses too early in the game (we usually start with greens and work up in a new club), I bet about $75 off the top. The deck stayed negative and I stayed with the green chips, betting as little as $25 per hand.

Finally, a deck went positive and I'd lost all of my green chips. Then the act began. A flush came over my face as I "nervously" reached into my pocket and pulled out a wad of $100 bills. I said to myself (but loudly enough so the bosses watching the game could think they were overhearing), "Sonofabitch—I got to get that money back."

I threw three $100 bills on the betting square, shaking my head and sighing as if to communicate, "Goddam it, here I go again — losing control and steaming."

I lost the hand. The count went up. My face got redder. I swore more and got my hands to shake nervously even more noticeably. I pulled out more bills and threw them recklessly on the square, sighing again and saying, "Bet the sonofabitch." At this point, there is no way a shuffle is going to take place. The dealer and boss have seen "steamers" over and over again—they lose control, they chase, they lose their heads. If the dealer were to shuffle, the 45 seconds or so might be enough of a delay to have this "steamer" come to his senses.

Yes, I lost that hand, too, and the count stayed up. At this point, there was only a quarter of a deck left. I hesitated—the dealer made no move to shuffle. I swore again, reached into my pocket, pulled out the whole sheaf of bills (about $5,000) and said, "How much can I bet?" (I knew, of course, that the Hilton had a $1,000 limit, but I was acting the out-of-control crazed steamer.)

The boss told me the limit. I threw out a stack of the bills (probably 14 or 15) and said, "Go ahead—if I lose, take 10." And then

I looked down, flushed, disgusted, and depressed as if I'd lost my month's pay.

It turned out that I won the $1,000 bet. I pulled the bills and chips back, breathed a sign of relief and, as the dealer shuffled, I "regained control," and bet $100 off the top.

"But," you'll say, "you can only do that when you are losing." Right indeed, and I must inform you that the times several consecutive losses come up in positive decks are all too distressing. If you can use that approach perhaps just every fourth or fifth session (where, as in this case, the ratio was 40-to-1), you're well ahead of the game. There are obviously similar approaches when you are see-sawing with the house, or winning big, which I'll leave to your imagination.

A few final points. If you have a sixteen and hit and bust and notice that the pit boss is watching you and wondering if you're a counter, make sure he notices that you look away immediately after you bust. You have no apparent interest in the dealer's hole card. Do that a few times and you'll convince him you're not counting. Sure, you'll miss the value of one or two cards occasionally. But, the trade-off is that you may get one or two more rounds dealt to you for hours.

When you're ahead, you should act happy, but also a little surprised as if it doesn't happen that often. When you're losing, don't act as if it's a rare occurrence. Do NOT assume that your losses will protect you from detection. Some of our greatest heat has come when we were losing. For one thing, there is a tendency to stay in the same club too long and become more aggressive in playing or in betting ratios, in an attempt to "dig out."

## WHAT TO DO IF YOU GET BARRED

As a precaution, you should always carry identification. There's no way in the world you can be arrested if you have ID. Without ID, the Nevada Metro Police can detain you on a formality. Two of our counters, neither with ID, were arrested.

You do not have to show your ID to casino personnel. If the casino people detain you and ask for your ID (they will act as if you must show it), you have merely to say, COURTEOUSLY, "I have identification, sir, but I would rather not show it to you. I'll just leave."

Some clubs like to take photos, authorized or unauthorized. The El Cortez once tried to take my picture. I replied, "I'll have to talk to my lawyer before I can authorize the photo." The picture-taking session never got off the ground.

Harrah's Tahoe, the Mint, and the Sands are also into photography. Resorts International has a photographic dossier of many card-counters taken through those dozens of bubbles dotting the casino ceiling.

If you're barred, the best thing to do is to quietly cash in your chips and leave. If you can get away without revealing your name, better yet. Play the other clubs. In six months of so, you'll be right back in the original club, probably on another shift. A barring is far from permanent; casino personnel change, people forget faces, you can grow a moustache, etc.

## LAWSUITS

My lawsuit against Resorts International went all the way to the New Jersey Supreme Court who decided in my favor. Several of the other cases filed in Federal Court (in both California and Nevada) have been dismissed, without the merits of the cases being considered for various reasons.

# CHAPTER THIRTEEN

# HOW TO BECOME AN EXPERT PLAYER

## by STANLEY ROBERTS

### UP THROUGH THE SKILL LEVELS

I suppose strictly speaking there are seven levels of Blackjack play. They are: The Unskilled Player, The Skilled Player (aware of the rules, but using no system), The Basic Strategy Player, The Intermediate Level Player, The Advanced Level Player, The Professional Level Player, and The Expert Level Player.

The Basic Strategy Player has about an even money chance—wins a few, loses a few. The Intermediate Level Player uses Basic Strategy and one simple count system. The Advanced Level Player uses Basic Strategy, a simple count system and an ace or 10-count. The Professional Level Player uses all of that plus a true count which he or she arrives at using a matrix. The Expert Level Player uses several counts, plus a true count, and does it all very well.

Not everyone is capable of using an Expert Level system. You need an excellent memory, a mathematical bent, an adequate bankroll, a good betting strategy and the ability to blend into the casino crowds.

Every Expert Level Player started at the Basic Strategy Level. But not every Basic Strategy Player can become an Expert Level Player. So, you need to work up through each level, and you will know when you've reached your limit. Whatever level you stop at past Basic Strategy gives you an edge against the house.

This book teaches you Basic Strategy and discusses card counting and higher skill levels. After you read and use this information, your next step is to read one or more of the following books. Many of these are available from *Gambling Times* magazine.

## BOOKS TO READ

The following 19 books (all of which appear in the Bibliography at the end of the book) are the best books written on Blackjack. We have listed them chronologically so that you can follow the winning strategies from the beginning.

1962/1969 BEAT THE DEALER by Edward O. Thorp, Ph.D.
Dr. Edward O. Thorp, Professor of Mathematics at the University of California at Irvine, first published his strategy for winning Blackjack in 1962. Using articles by Baldwin, et al, and Julian Braun, Dr. Thorp developed his system through mathematics and checked it with an electronic computer. When the paperback edition was published in 1962, Las Vegas Blackjack rules were changed drastically. Subsequently, in 1969 Dr. Thorp revised his point count system and showed the player how to win in spite of the rule changes. An excellent book—the basic tenets in this book presented material that was used in one form or another by most other authors of Blackjack books.

1971/1981 WINNING BLACKJACK by Stanley Roberts
Stanley Roberts stopped playing Blackjack when it wasn't any fun anymore. He had won more money than he would need for a long, long time; the challenge was gone and his interest waned. It was at this point that he decided to write his first book. It proved to be a tremendous success—financially, no other Blackjack book has made more money. Stanley Roberts, in addition to setting forth a Basic Strategy, offers a Ten-Count Strategy that

has the ease and simplicity of any other point count system. Included in the book, are photos showing the many ways a dealer can cheat a player. The book is written in an easy-to-read style and shows the player how to win at Blackjack whether one, two or more decks are used. A second edition of *Winning Blackjack* was published in 1981.

### 1973 HOW TO WIN AT WEEKEND BLACKJACK by Stanley Roberts

Here again Stanley Roberts gives the player the inside story of just what goes on in the gambling casino, information about the owners, the pit bosses, the dealers and the shills. But, most important, the focus of this book is how you, the player, can get the casino to play your game, instead of your playing their game. The book describes in detail everything the player needs to know about the game of Blackjack. The rules of the game, the proper playing strategy, using your knowledge of what has transpired to increase your percentage edge over the casino, and the important points about how not to get barred from the casino are all here in this book. (Currently out of print.)

### 1973 PLAYING BLACKJACK AS A BUSINESS by Lawrence Revere

Lawrence Revere, who was a pit boss, dealer, trouble shooter and professional Blackjack player for twenty-seven years, finally wrote a book outlining the Blackjack system he used to win. And win he did; for nine years, he lived entirely on his Blackjack winnings. His method consists of a multiple-strategy concept. It's simple; his book is easy to read and includes graphs and charts to help in the learning process. His system was exhaustively cross-checked and tested with computers by Julian Braun of IBM. Revere's claim was: If you seriously apply the instructions given in his book, you will no longer be gambling when you play Blackjack. You will be in business!

1975 THE DEVELOPMENT AND ANALYSIS OF WINNING STRATEGIES FOR THE CASINO GAME OF BLACKJACK by Julian H. Braun

Julian Braun, M.S., of IBM Corporation, enjoys that rare distinction of being universally regarded as one of the world's foremost authorities in the field of computer analyses of Blackjack probabilities. His research over the past twenty-four years gives him an expertise and knowledge of the subject which is unparalled. Roberts calls Braun "...the germinator of nearly all Blackjack systems." Thorp claims that "Julian Braun has transformed my original Blackjack computer program into the world's most powerful and accurate tool for the calculation of winning Blackjack strategies." Julian Braun's interest and love of Blackjack dates back to the 1950's and he wants to share his love of the game with others. This book helps him do it and will help the reader who is ready to win at the game of Blackjack!

1977 BLACKJACK YOUR WAY TO RICHE$ by Robert Albert Canfield

Robert Canfield (a pseudonym for a Las Vegas pit boss and four of the most successful Blackjack players in the world) has written a book that is virtually a one volume course in the successful technique of playing winning Blackjack. You will learn how it is possible to win at the rate of your choice—from merely paying for a vacation to moving into a six-figure bracket. This book teaches you money management, the right method of preserving and building your capital, including details on bet size, tipping, fluctuation, credit, junkets, taxes and much more. The authors have thorough answers to the toughest questions you might have. They tell you why the game will thrive and survive, they give you a full analysis of counters, cheaters, casinos barring players and countless other pointers. Whether you are a casual amateur or a serious professional, you will want to take advantage of the edge this book can give you.

1977 THE BIG PLAYER by Ken Uston with Roger Rapaport

From March 1974 to June 1976 a team of Blackjack experts raked off over $1,000,000 from the tables of Las Vegas and various casinos in Europe and South America. They used a unique system where groups of card counters, stationed at several tables and placing minimum bets, kept track of the value of the cards dealt and then called in the roving Big Player when the decks turned "hot"— rich with high cards and aces. The Big Player then put huge amounts into "action" often betting the house limit at the hot table.

Ken Uston, the senior vice president of the Pacific Stock Exchange, was one of the Big Players recruited for this team. The experiences of the team are told in this book. It is a lucid and funny account of what all gamblers dream of—a successful plan for beating the house—and of the fantasy life of the Las Vegas high roller. (Currently out of print.)

1979 BLACKJACK SUPER GOLD by Lance Humble, Ph.D.

Dr. Humble claims that this book is the first book that actually teaches you how to win money playing Blackjack in a casino— even under adverse conditions. This book also teaches you how to play a simple winning strategy against any number of decks; how to slow down a fast dealer; five wagering methods to suit all conditions; when to bet a lot, when to bet the minimum, when to quit; how to avoid getting barred; and lastly, how to play like a professional. The Introduction and two sections in the book are written by Julian Braun and the Foreword is written by Dr. Edward O. Thorp. The methods Dr. Humble gives in his book have won the author and his students over half a million dollars in just four years. (Currently out of print.)

1980 THE WORLD'S GREATEST BLACKJACK BOOK by Lance Humble, Ph.D. and Carl Cooper, Ph.D.

According to Drs. Humble and Cooper, they have written the most comprehensive book ever published on Blackjack. Humble and Cooper (two university professors) have proven in actual play that a knowledgeable Blackjack player has an advantage over the house. This book is actually three books in one: the definitive Basic Strategy for playing the cards; the first introduction to the general public of the powerful simple betting system HI-OPT I; and a readable, enjoyable, and complete guide to casino play around the world.

1980 THE BLACKJACK FORMULA by Arnold Snyder
This book, according to the author, is to be used as a guide. Used properly, it will give the serious Blackjack player a method of determining his or her advantage in any particular game. A pocket calculator with keys for using parentheses and for finding square roots would be a wise investment. If you follow the math with your own calculations, it should not be difficult. The book contains no system, nor is it a primer. The reader should be familiar with common Blackjack terminology. The first chapter explains the concept of standard deviation for those who may not be familiar with it. The remainder of the book, supplemented by the Appendix, reveals a formula which is referred to as the BLACKJACK FORMULA.

1980 HOW TO PLAY WINNING BLACKJACK by Julian Braun
Julian Braun's name and his work have been quoted in over a dozen books and in countless articles. He has written this book to "set the record straight." Also, he is a devoted Blackjack player and is hoping that the readers of his book find his devotion contagious and that these same readers will benefit from the ideas and observations outlined in the book. Braun attempts to trace his work over the last eighteen years in a logical manner. In so doing, he crystalizes and supports the foundation of the Basic Strategy charts contained in his book, particularly in the area of the four- or six-deck games. Braun, whose avocation continues to be Blackjack research, finds great joy in what he does and this latest book outlines for the serious player the things that Braun has found to be valuable and profitable for him.

**1980 MILLION DOLLAR BLACKJACK by Ken Uston**
Ken Uston brings to the reader a broad range of Blackjack systems, from a handful of rules for the lazy player, which will surely cut his losses, to the most efficient Professional-level system, which should only be undertaken by the serious and experienced player. Included are basic strategies for all major casino areas as well as Intermediate-level, Advanced-level, beginning Professional-level and advanced Professional-level strategies. The reader is cautioned that he or she should not expect an instant injection of Blackjack wisdom just from reading this book. Uston's experiences playing Blackjack are liberally sprinkled throughout the book. He relates how he chose and trained members of his now-famous Blackjack teams, and what happened at the casinos in which they played. This is the most comprehensive and most powerful book ever published on the game of Blackjack.

**1981 BLACKJACK FOR PROFIT by Arnold Snyder**
This is a little book—less than 100 pages and only 4″ x 5″ in size. It is a guide for card counters and evaluates the most common games in Las Vegas, Reno-Lake Tahoe area, and Atlantic City. It explains how much money you need to play, how much you can expect to win (or lose), and how to decide which counting system is best for you. The book provides a simple point method called, *The Snyder Profit Index,* which you can use to evaluate the profit potential of any game quickly and easily.

**1982 BLACKJACK'S WINNING FORMULA by Jerry Patterson**
This book presents specific information on how to play the game (and *win!*) plus the four-part winning formula that changes the odds to favor the player, not the dealer, regardless of which rules are used. With step-by-step instructions in card counting and detailed information to help players decide how to bet and when

to fold, this book explains how to play the different worldwide variants of the game. Now expanded with special chapters by world famous Dominic, this book is a must for anyone who plans to make money at casino resorts in Atlantic City, Nevada or the Caribbean.

1982 BLACKJACK: A WINNER'S HANDBOOK by Jerry Patterson

This book was written to satisfy the needs of the occasional gambler as he confronts these myriad systems and the large body of scientific research about the game. This book helps the occasional gambler to select the Blackjack system that he or she is capable of learning and that best suits his or her style of play, the time he or she wishes to invest, and the risk he or she wishes to take. It offers the beginning player a simplified winning system based on 9 BILLION hands of computer-played Blackjack. It offers the intermediate player a step-by-step approach to becoming an advanced player based on an analysis of 50 Blackjack systems. It offers the advanced player a recommendation for an advanced system which will maximize his or her winnings. For the occasional player, this book will serve as a complete, self-contained handbook.

1983 CASINO GAMBLING: WINNING TECHNIQUES FOR CRAPS, ROULETTE, BLACKJACK AND BACCARAT by Jerry Patterson and Walter Jaye

This book offers proven techniques players can use to reduce house odds, and in some cases turn the odds in their own favor, for four popular table games: Craps, Roulette, Baccarat and Blackjack. This book covers subjects other than Blackjack, but it does include a section on tournament strategies. An excellent beginner's primer for all four games.

1983 BLACKBELT IN BLACKJACK by Arnold Snyder

The subtitle of this book is "Playing 21 as a Martial Art." Many of the same talents, skills and virtues which would earn you a top ranking position in any of the martial arts can also be applied to casino Blackjack. The concept of card counting is based on *balance,* and making your attack when you are in the stronger position. You never make yourself vulnerable to your opponent (the casino), but through your superior knowledge of your opponent's weaknesses (rules, conditions, cards remaining to be played, etc.), you allow your opponent to bring about his own loss. Your strategy is based on *simplicity,* not complexity. You take no foolish chances. What moves you make are made with precision, with force ($), and perfect timing. Your opponent thinks he can beat you, thinks he *is* beating you, and does not see the strength of your superior position. You make your moves with a natural ease. Your camouflage, which allows you to win, is your ability to appear as if you are not even trying. Snyder recognizes that many of his readers will go on to become masters of Blackjack strategy, so his book offers many simplified, albeit less powerful, methods that the casual player may use to better his or her chances of winning at the Blackjack tables.

1984 THE BEGINNER'S GUIDE TO WINNING BLACK-JACK by Stanley Roberts
The world's leading Blackjack writer (and world-class player) has written a book especially for beginners to the game. This book tells how to obtain an instant advantage through the simplest of techniques. It is written in an easy-to-read style and shows you how to win at all games of casino Blackjack, regardless of the number of decks used. Roberts covers the history of the game, the rules of casino Blackjack, the art of casino play and many more subjects. Bankrolling and betting strategy are covered in depth, and charts and tables show you visually what is discussed in print. At the back of the book there is a study section that teaches Basic Strategy, an Ace Count, a Five Count, a Combination Ace-Five Count, a HI-OPT Count and four lessons on simulated and actual casino play for both single-deck and multi-

deck play. Flash Cards and a Quiz are also included. This book is probably the most complete text written for the beginner player who wants to become an intermediate player.

1984 MATHEMATICS OF GAMBLING by Edward O. Thorp, Ph.D.

Thorp's first book, *Beat the Dealer,* set the gambling world on fire. Casinos started running scared. They increased the number of decks used; they made crazy rule changes; and in the process almost killed the game of Blackjack. However, some sense of sanity soon prevailed and the game once again came alive and sparked the interest of Blackjack players around the world. Thorp, with the publication of his first book in 1962, finally convinced the populace what the experienced Blackjack player knew all along: A knowledgeable Blackjack player can have an edge against the house! Now, at last, Thorp has written a second book not only on Blackjack but on Baccarat, The Wheel of Fortune, Roulette, Backgammon and Horse Racing. He discusses the mathematical odds on each game and optimal betting strategies. The "Albert Einstein" of gambling has done it again!

# CHAPTER FOURTEEN

# YOUR BANKROLL

## by STANLEY ROBERTS

This chapter deals with what it's all about—MONEY. How much you need to start and how to use it are the subjects of this section. We will also discuss the critical factor of the Gambler's Ruin Problem.

Basically speaking, a bankroll is the *total* amount of money that you will commit to Blackjack play for an extended period of time. It is not the amount that you will wager, nor is it the amount you will be carrying around with you from casino to casino. It is the total amount of money that *could* be used if it were necessary.

The principle that one must rigidly exercise in casino play is: NEVER play with scared money. This means that you should never play with money that you cannot afford to lose. The psychological effect of playing with scared money is such that most of the benefits of any system will be nullified. The frightened player makes mistakes, gives himself away as a system player, fails to act boldly when he should, thus reducing his proper percentage plays.

Always keep your living expenses separated from your playing bankroll. Never try to use your bankroll for daily living expenses. Only use money that you have deemed excess—money that you can afford to lose. This will usually be savings of some sort that you have managed to accumulate beyond your normal needs.

Once again: Bankroll money is NOT next month's car payment or your wife's birthday present money, and it is certainly NOT your emergency money. You must provide for these things first so that you will be able to play coolly and confidently. Lastly, bankroll money ought to be considered speculative money that could grow very quickly into a sizable sum, given a sufficient amount of time and correct play.

## HOW TO GET YOUR MONEY

Playing capital can come from savings, trade-off expenses, or from free money that the casinos and others give away.

A number of agencies give free money, free meals and free playing dollars to encourage people to use their facilities. These "goodies," as they are often referred to, may be obtained in a number of ways. Don't be afraid to ask about them everyplace you go.

CASINOS: Many casinos have their own special giveaway programs. Simply ask the cashiers, room clerks or other casino personnel about what is currently being given away.

MOTELS: Most of the motels have a broad, if not complete, selection of goodies that are given out on a daily basis to each guest over 21 years of age.

NEWSPAPERS: The local newspapers, particularly those that specialize in entertainment news, usually have coupons printed in them for some goodie or another or they direct you where to go to get that goodie.

LAND PROMOTIONS: Several major land developers are giving away meals and gambling money if you will only listen to their presentation. Ask about them and you will find them. They usually advertise in the local entertainment paper.

TOURS: Certain bus companies, or chartered junkets, have their own special coupons that can be obtained for taking their tours.

SALES PROMOTERS: Several agencies are involved in the

giving away of coupons to out-of-town visitors. These can be found advertised in the local papers or the major newspapers in the Los Angeles, San Francisco, New York and New Jersey areas.

FREE GAS: Some casinos will reimburse you with playing money for your gasoline expenses. These may usually be found advertised in local papers or the major newspapers in the cities and states noted above.

If you would have spent money on meals or drinks that you can get free for tickets, then consider this a savings which you can add to your original stake.

After you have built your gambling bankroll to an adequate size, you will find that it is no longer profitable for you to waste this time collecting goodies since you can win more money by simply playing Blackjack in the time it would take you to collect the goodies. For the player who has no money to risk, this is a good way to start. For those players who have money to risk, it is a waste of time. It is better to feel that you are playing with "their money," but remember, once it is in your pocket, it is your money.

## GAMBLER'S RUIN

There will be times when you will not lose one single hand out of twenty. You will seem to be unbeatable. Likewise, there will be times when it will seem like you should have stayed in bed! What gamblers call "streaks" are nothing more than backward glances at probability to a mathematician. They can and will occur during any short-term period. To prevent a bad series from wiping out your bankroll you will have to exercise self-control and rigidly follow proper bankrolling rules.

One of the best ways to avoid Gambler's Ruin is to divide your bankroll into ten equal parts, each of which is called a "mini-bank." At NO time will you permit more than one of these mini-banks to be lost at one table. If you should drop that mini-bank, then pick up and leave.

Do NOT allow your playing to become a personal ego struggle with any particular dealer or casino. You must lose occasionally.

Take that loss gracefully like a pro.

If you ever run into a dealer who remarks that he is "hot" (or something to that effect), or, if he says he has been beating them all day, believe him—don't play with him. Probability is a funny bird. It runs in streaks more often than not. When this happens—COOL IT. Take a walk, leave, get out, eat lunch, take a break, but stop playing.

We could devote an entire page to this next phrase; we probably should. Let it suffice just once: "When you are cold, cool off."

With an unlimited bankroll, there is no chance of ruination (losing your entire bankroll), and we could express your chances of ruination mathematically as 0%. With an extremely large bankroll and a very small maximum bet, our chances for losing the entire bankroll might be about 0.00000001% (still practically zero). The trick is to find an acceptable level of risk with a given sum of money and as large a maximum bet as is "safe."

There are three bankrolling combinations that will be described for your consideration. Each has a different ruination factor listed as a percentage. A 10% ruination means that there is a 10% chance of losing your entire bankroll. Obviously, the lower the percent ruination factor, the "safer" it is.

## TABLE 14-1

> ### BANKROLLING METHOD 1
>
> 5 times Maximum Bet=Mini-Bank
> 10 times Mini-Bank=Playing Bank (Bankroll)
> 5% Ruination
> With a total bankroll of $2,000 each mini-bank (10%) is $200 and the maximum bet would be $40 (5 times 40=200).

## TABLE 14-2

---

### BANKROLLING METHOD 2

10 times Maximum Bet=Mini-Bank
10 times Mini-Bank=Total Playing Bank (Bankroll)
1% Ruination

---

## TABLE 14-3

---

### BANKROLLING METHOD 3

Maximum Bet=Total Playing Bank (Bankroll)÷100
Mini-Bank=10% of Bankroll
0.001% Ruination

---

Method 3 is basically the same as Method 2. The difference is that the maximum bet is *always* held to 1% of the bankroll. For example, with a $2,000 Playing Bank, the maximum bet is $20, the same as Method 2. However, if the bankroll drops to, say, $1,900, the maximum bet becomes $19.

Similarly, if the bankroll increases to $2,100, the maximum bet becomes $21. Mini-banks become 10% of the entire bankroll at the time they are used. A mini-bank from a $2,500 bankroll is $250, while later on in the playing session a mini-bank might become $300 (10% of $3,000). Because the bet size decreases if the bankroll is decreased, the ruination factor is a low 0.001%. This is the safest of the three methods.

Methods 1 and 2 are significantly more risky (a calculated risk, not a gamble) than Method 3, and they really should only be used by more aggressive players or those who wish to build up from a small bankroll as quickly as possible. Once a bankroll of one to two thousand dollars has been reached, Method 3 becomes more and more attractive.

## HOW TO USE YOUR MONEY

The term "unit" is generally taken to mean the size of your minimum bet or, perhaps, the size of the casino chips that you are using. Thus, if you were playing with red chips, $5, your unit would be $5. Green chips are $25. Tokens are usually made of metal and have replaced the silver dollars now out of general circulation. Your unit could be an odd number as well; possibly $2.50, $3.00, $6.00 or any basic minimum bet that you choose.

Ideally, a player would realize an enormous advantage if he were to play only when the deck becomes favorable and sit out those hands when the deck becomes poor. This practice works particularly well in the multiple-deck games which tend to hold a rich or poor pattern over a longer period of time. This practice, when used too often, will give away your style of play.

The next best thing to sitting out poor deck conditions is to have as wide a unit spread between the table minimum and what your bankroll will allow as a maximum. Generally, a ten-unit spread is desired. For example, with a bankroll of $2,000 using Method 2, your maximum bet size would be $20. To achieve a ten-unit spread, your minimum bet would have to be $2. It should be obvious that if you were playing at a $5 minimum table, your unit spread would only be four units (4 times $5 = $20). You must coordinate your bankroll with your betting so that your maximum bet is ten times the size of your minimum bet.

Once you have set your maximum bet, NEVER change it during that session. To do so borders on gambling. The practice of increasing one's bet constantly, especially on a losing streak, is referred to as "steaming." Steaming is usually accompanied by increased frustration and turning red in the face.

Let us repeat this point for emphasis: NEVER EXCEED YOUR MAXIMUM BET. This does not apply to splitting pairs or doubling down when you have made a maximum bet; naturally, you must split and double as your playing strategy indicates.

Avoid entering the game in the middle of a shuffle, unless you have been counting from the beginning. When you do not know the count, wait until the deck is reshuffled. After the reshuffle, don't always make your new bet only one unit. If you start with a big bet at a new table or after a reshuffle, your other betting patterns will confuse the dealer. Most people start out with a small bet to get the feel of things. Because you know that you have the edge with a complete deck, make a four- to six-unit bet. It is easy to pull back your level later without raising any suspicion.

At all times, it is best to be deceptive about your incremental increases in betting. One way to do this is by not always using one chip (either $1, $5, or $25) as your minimum bet. Also, try acting a little bit. If you are not a professional, be careful not to overdo it. Show mild anger when you lose and mild delight when you win, as if to say, "How lucky I am." Be sure that you don't delude yourself into thinking that it is a matter of "luck."

## HOW TO PROTECT YOUR MONEY

Concealing your winnings is a very important part of your playing method. Always try to give the impression of being just one of the other suckers, a loser. As mentioned before, don't place a large amount of money in front of you right away. Give the impression of continually having to dig for more money.

As you begin to win and accumulate a stack of chips, begin to remove some without any fanfare (and preferably when no one is looking), and slip them in your pocket or purse. Of course, don't be obvious about what you are doing; act nonchalantly. If you need more money, don't go for the chips; cash in some more bills.

The floorman is careful to observe the dealer's rack to see that it is full. Do not win too much from any one table because you will be noticed. Move your action around and take a little bit from each of the tables. When you do stack your chips on the table, place small chips on top of big ones. If the floorman only glances in your direction, he will think that you have less. Don't stack up your chips too neatly. It makes it easier for them to count your winnings.

## THE IMPORTANCE OF ATTITUDE

At this point, we hope we've convinced you that the game of Blackjack can be beaten. The question is, "Can you do it?" Let us assure you that, if you've managed to come this far in the book, you have the ability to do so. If the terms and expressions used here are unfamiliar to you, and the concepts are new, do not be disheartened. A little time (and the Glossary at the back of the book) will make it all quite clear!

It has been our experience that success in an endeavor in life is more a question of attitude than anything else, surpassing knowledge, experience, and money. If, on the one hand, you believe that you can succeed, you have a good chance of doing so, provided you are willing to make the necessary effort.

The principal ingredient in learning to use and profit from any system is DISCIPLINE. Your play must be disciplined, in line with the instructions presented. However, it must not appear to be disciplined to the casual observant casino personnel.

Speaking of attitude—what is the attitude of the casino? What they want is simply to relieve you of your money, smoothly and without any complaints. To do this they will distract you, wear you down, get you drunk, exert pressure on you with dirty or suspicious looks from floormen and pit bosses, or make you feel guilty for winning.

Since you are aware of what they have in mind, and·you now know that you have the knowledge and ability to beat them, you should have an attitude of CONFIDENCE. You can WIN. You will win. Hold these thoughts foremost in your mind. With this attitude you are now prepared to beat them NOT at their game, but at YOUR game.

# CHAPTER FIFTEEN

# TOURNAMENT PLAY

## by STANLEY ROBERTS

For years now, the casino marketing departments have been trying to bring in large groups of people through the convention process. This process fills the rooms, and hopefully some of the conventioneers will be players. However, the convention does bring its own competing meeting and show schedules which keep the players out of the casino.

But a gaming tournament—more specifically, a Blackjack tournament—is like having a gambling convention with the main meeting right in the casino.

## MAJOR AND MINOR LEAGUE TOURNAMENTS

There seem to be two kinds of events shaping up—major and minor league tournaments. The principal differences between the two are the buy-in and the prize structure. The minor events generally have a $100 entry fee, a $250 buy-in and a prize structure in the $25,000-to-$50,000 area. The major events have a $250 entry fee, a $500-$600 buy-in and a $75,000-plus prize pool. The major league events require a considerable amount of coordination and marketing and are usually handled by outside consultants. Major events are currently held at the Desert Inn, Harrah's and the Tropicana.

With the exception of the Desert Inn, all of the events are run on a table elimination basis. The Desert Inn format has been copyrighted by its creators, Casino Marketing International.

## THE HISTORY OF BLACKJACK TOURNAMENTS

As early as December 1978, an organization called, "World Championship of Blackjack, Inc." (WCB) with some difficulty persuaded the management of the Las Vegas Sahara to hold a tournament. It was highly successful drawing about 1400 entries. It's success was due in part to our endorsement and the endorsement of *Gambling Times* Magazine.

The WCB Blackjack tournaments use the table elimination format and one has to concentrate on the five other players at one's table. The object here is not necessarily to win but to end up with more money than the five others at your table. In other words, the goal could easily be—lose the least amount of money and you'll be a winner. The proper strategy for this format is quite easy to figure out: Conserve your bankroll until the last few hands. However, do not allow any particular opponent to get so far ahead that your chances for the win are too slim. When someone gains on the pack, you must narrow the gap to keep within striking distance.

It is quite common in this type of event to see minimum bets until the last five minutes of play, with a flurry of major—even total bankroll or table maximum—bets at the end.

The innovative, unique, non-elimination format created by Casino Marketing International (CMI) ends the unpopular war of attrition on players. Entrants can choose to compete in round-after-round of open play even if their earlier Blackjack play was unlucky. These same players can stay in the running for a major cash prize or other valuable awards. Using the CMI tournament format, players are not eliminated by the droves at the end of each round as they are in WCB tournaments.

In the non-elimination format the least loser will not win the tournament. This may even be one of the prime benefits of this event—one has to be a winner, to BE a winner! Although there are rewards for winning at your table, including a new high-scoring Triple Table Winner entry to the Championship Playoff, the real rewards come from building up the highest final bank that you can achieve in 100 hands.

Round Winner—those with the highest total in each round—get cash prizes AND entry to the Championship Playoff. So, too, does the one player who has achieved the highest total in all three rounds: the Cumulative Table Winner.

Since each round is composed of several sessions, those persons who have the highest total in their session (generally among 120 players), have the opportunity to play off for the final seat at the Championship Playoff Table.

## WHO SHOULD PLAY TOURNAMENT BLACKJACK

If you are a professional Blackjack player—one who earns his living at the game—it probably is not in your own best interest to play in Blackjack tournaments. Your livelihood depends upon your anonymity and your low-profile playing. Each year media coverage of these Blackjack tournaments grows larger and larger—and winners become instantly recognized.

The winners of these Blackjack tournaments are usually people who use good basic strategy, understand money management and betting, and who are "lucky" that particular day. We don't mean to down-play skill. In the long run, the skill factor can certainly influence the game in your favor. So, the question remains: Is the risk of exposure worth the prize money? Only you can answer that question.

## TOURNAMENT PROCEDURES

Since procedures differ between the WCB format and the CMI format, we will give them both.

All players must be officially registered prior to the start of the tournament. Blackjack tables and starting times are randomly assigned. All tournament rounds either last two hours or have a fixed number of hands to be played.

There are usually three rounds of play (called the preliminary rounds), plus the Championship Playoff round. At the beginning of each preliminary round, players buy-in for a stipulated amount—usually from $250 on up to $600. The players receive special tournament chips in exchange for their cash buy-in. No additional buy-ins are allowed for that round.

In the WCB format, at the end of a two-hour period, the player with the most money is declared the winner for that table and advances to the next round. The other players are eliminated.

There are additional rounds of elimination play. Although it depends on the total number of players enrolled in the WCB tournament, usually six players play at the first three rounds, and usually seven players compete at each table in the semi-final round. In the final round, only three players compete with each other. The player who holds the most money at the end of the final round is declared the Champion and is awarded the prize money.

In the CMI format, after one hundred hands have been dealt, the player with the most money wins the round. That player receives $12,000, and advances to the next round. Second and third also receive cash prizes. All table winners then advance to the next round; however losers can re-enter and play the second round by paying a reduced entry fee and all play for a $15,000 prize with second and third cash prizes.

In round three, the same procedure is followed except the prize money jumps to $18,000. The person who wins the largest cumulative total for all three rounds wins a luxury automobile. This person does not necessarily have to be a round winner. Travel awards are given at the end of each round as runner-up prizes

The CMI tournament format provides for the qualification of a maximum of six in the championship round. They are: the winners of each of the three rounds, the player with the highest cumulative win over all three round, the Triple Table Winner with the highest total score, and the player who wins the Session Winners Playoff round. The winner of this final round receives $75,000.

## HOW TO PLAY TOURNAMENT BLACKJACK

Players who enter the tournament should adopt a focused view of their purpose—the only reason you are there is to win. If you just want to play Blackjack at your own pace and without the constraints of the rules of tournament play, you shouldn't be there.

Once that fact is established, you should be prepared to risk your entire stake at the appropriate time if there is any feasible way that you can win the round. If it is clear to you that you're out, you should withdraw from play and save your remaining chips for a later time.

There are three major factors that will affect the outcome. These are luck, betting strategy or money management, and skill—in that order. Since luck is not a factor we can measure, we can deal only with the other variables.

Although there are seven levels, ranging from totally unskilled to expert, for the purpose of this discussion we will refer to tournament players as unskilled, Basic Strategy players, or skilled players. It is unlikely that someone who does not play close to Basic Strategy (or better) will win the tournament.

There are times when the correct strategy, be it basic or expert, becomes subject to exceptions to the rule. These exceptions will invariably involve the last hand or two. For example, in one dramatic play, a heads-up player was dealt a Blackjack on the final hand. Her payoff would have left her without sufficient sums to beat one other opponent. She alertly doubled-down on the Blackjack, thereby winning the hand and the round. Of course, one doesn't need a Blackjack to do this. You can double-down on any two cards, even a hard 19, should that be your only way to win.

## GENERAL GUIDELINES

Do not drink alcoholic beverages before or during the time you are playing. You want to be as physically and mentally alert as possible. Refrain from all excesses and that includes overeating, little or no sleep, etc.

Remember that you are out to beat your opponents. Be pleasant, but not friendly. Don't do anything to break your concentration. You are out to WIN!

In a WCB tournament, do not toke the dealers until the round is over and all the chips have been counted. You could toke yourself right out of the prize money.

Be aware of the time or number of hands left to play in each round. This is particularly important in the final hour.

If you are lucky enough to stay in the contest until the end, you should be very aware of the amount of money each of the remaining players has. You must know how much money you have also. Your final bets must anticipate the end results so you have to keep your mind alert and your eye keen. Many people have lost their rounds by making an insufficent bet or by making too large a bet at the end.

Blackjack tournaments are fun-filled, exciting times that may possibly lead to big money for the disciplined, Basic Strategy player who has a nodding acquaintance wtih Lady Luck!

# CHAPTER SIXTEEN

# PROTECTING THE GAME

## by STANLEY ROBERTS

In the last several years, we have witnessed a remarkable growth in the gaming industry. Blackjack is increasing at the rate of 50% faster than all the gambling games played in casinos. Why is this so? It has come about because of player interest in the game of Blackjack. More and more people have come to believe that they have a good shot at winning at the Blackjack table, and so they're willing to take the risk of playing the game. And the people who are really responsible for this growth are the authors who have written books on the subject of Blackjack. These authors are (or were) themselves players of Blackjack—players who were also winners at the game. When Dr. Edward O. Thorp's book, *Beat the Dealer,* first came out, the Nevada casinos starting making ridiculous rule changes that almost killed the game of Blackjack. People stayed away from the Blackjack tables by the thousands. They were getting the message that the casinos were sending out: We are only interested in losers—no winners allowed! When the casinos realized their mistake, the rules were adjusted and players once again flocked to the Blackjack tables.

But the casinos still didn't want any card counters playing so they started barring people who were winning what they thought was too much money. At this point, the casinos became vulnerable and as many of you know, Ken Uston, who was barred from Resorts International in Atlantic City, New Jersey, took Resorts to court, lost at the local level, but persevered and appealed to the New Jersey State Supreme Court and WON. Some players were finally starting to fight back.

## HOW TO COMPLAIN

If at all possible, try to get a complaint handled at the pit boss level or at the shift manager level. Sometimes, of course, this is not possible to do because you may not get any satisfaction at this level. If this is the case, your only recourse is to make a complaint to the state agency that controls the casino industry. At this time, that would be the State of Nevada Gaming Control Board or the State of New Jersey Casino Control Commission.

These agencies receive an average of 10 to 15 complaints per month. These complaints may be filed in writing or by telephone. When a complaint is received, it is written up and investigated as soon as manpower will permit. An evaluation is then made and the complainant notified of the results. The number of investigating agents in Nevada are few, the licensees many, and most casinos operate three shifts; so it sometimes takes a long time for a complaint to be investigated. In New Jersey, each casino has a full complement of inspectors on hand during operating hours, but the number of licensees in New Jersey (currently 10) is far smaller than Nevada's (approximately 200).

The Board and the Commission represent the only "court of appeals" open to players in the settlement of disputes. Through recent legislation, gambling debts are now legally collectible, either by player or casino, and now can be a potential matter for civil litigation. The administrative power of these two state agencies give them the authority to settle players' claims. Furthermore, recent legislation in New Jersey made gaming debts secured by personal checks collectible.

Nevada casinos bar card counters from playing Blackjack even though they are not doing anything illegal or in bad taste—except, of course, *winning.* The position of the Nevada Board is that the casinos are in business to make money and those players who are good at the game of Blackjack (and are recognized as such by the house) can be barred from future play. Of course, we could state this another way and say that only those players who lose money are welcome to continue playing in Nevada. Card counters may NOT be barred in New Jersey.

If we look objectively at both state agencies to see if they will give your complaint a fair shake, we must recognize that as much as one third of those states' revenue comes from taxes on gambling. Further, a good portion of the remainder comes from taxes on industries, such as motels, restaurants, etc., that are only in operation due to the fact that people who have come to gamble also have other needs, such as food, clothing and shelter. If you were cheated in the casino, it would be your word against the dealer's and he or she would be backed up by a host of big businessmen who know the Governor and everybody else.

We believe that the state agencies try to do an honest job in keeping the games straight and the mobsters out. But with the limited staff available, it is hard to believe that this job can be done adequately. The best a player can do to protect him/herself is to play only in large casinos and bet modest sums (since, theoretically, there is too much at stake for the big casino to try to cheat a small-time player). Because the recognized, better Blackjack players are barred, and the rest of the games cannot be beaten mathematically, the only player who can make a profit in the casino is an *unrecognized,* skilled Blackjack player.

## THE ACHIEVEMENTS AND FAILURES OF THE NEVADA AND NEW JERSEY STATE AGENCIES

Gambling is "legal" in Nevada and in New Jersey and, therefore, each state exercises control over its operation. This gaming control is vested entirely in the hands of the Governors of these two States, and they alone appoint all the other officials.

The Nevada State Gaming Control Board has several years' more experience than the State of New Jersey Casino Control Commission. When the Nevada Board was created, outside of the guidelines set up by the state, they were traveling previously uncharted waters. When the New Jersey Commission was charged with its duties, it not only had that state's guidelines, but the past experiences of the Nevada Board to draw on.

The Nevada gaming experience has and is serving as a major source of experimental data for the formulation of legislation and control procedures by areas considering implementation of legalized casino gaming.

Las Vegas and Reno-Tahoe have experienced tremendous growth over the years. This growth and the success of the casinos are directly related to the way in which the Nevada Board operates. It is by no means perfect—what government agency is?—but it tries and while all change comes slowly, the Nevada Board, recognizing that it holds a unique role of leadership in the field of gambling, does make changes. Most of these changes benefit the gaming industry—some do not.

The New Jersey Casino Control Commission has now had five years to get its act together. The time of experimentation with the "new" gaming business of New Jersey must now come to an end. The maiden voyage should now be over and the "shaking out" process completed.

Specifically, the people of New Jersey, including the operators of casinos, should petition their legislature to conduct a review of the casino regulatory process, simplifying that process and removing many of the unnecessary burdens that have been placed upon the operators. Steps should be taken to reduce the power and authority of the Commission to more common sense principles and perfunctory simple administrative duties in order to allow the industry to grow properly and permit the standards of the marketplace to govern the activities of the gaming industry, much like the more mature Nevada example.

We have had the privilege of becoming close friends with many top-level executives in the casino industry. These include owners, chief executive officers, lawyers, casino managers, marketing directors and a host of other job titles. We have also been present at the birth and growth of the casino industry in New Jersey. What has become all too apparent to us is that the regulatory process from restrictive working conditions to ludicrous procedures is threatening to choke the gaming industry in New Jersey.

Some of this can be attributed to the immaturity of the process and the ignorance of the newly appointed regulators. However, as we mentioned above, that excuse has now run its course. The members of the Commission are all appointed officers. They have come to their office, not out of many years of experience in the field, but out of political favor. They may have the necessary character (and I don't doubt that they have), but surely they do not have the proper background.

Now we are left with the question: Who is to regulate the regulators? You must find that answer within yourself.

As additional states legalize casino gaming, competitive considerations should lead to correcting present deficiencies in both Nevada and New Jersey gaming conditions. Time is running out.

## WHY RULES AREN'T STANDARDIZED

Presently, we have casino gambling in only two states: Nevada and New Jersey. The governing agency for each of these states gives general guidelines within which each casino has the option to name its rules. Even in the same city, the rules can differ. How many decks used; how many cards to burn; where the burn card is placed; minimum bet allowed; maximum bet allowed; and on and on—and these rule discrepancies are only for the game of Blackjack!

As more and more states adopt legalized casino gambling, the rules for each game will tend to change and perhaps become more standardized. The casino player is fickle—he or she will play where the rules allow the player, if not a fighting chance, at least a fair game. A fair game means that the player while he or she may be losing money, does not feel cheated by the casino. In other words, players will not flock to casinos who gain the reputation of welcoming only losers. Once a casino gets a reputation like that, it's hard to change it.

In Chapter Seventeen, we outline suggested international rules for Blackjack. We feel it's the only way interest in the game will continue to grow. We also feel that it's the only way to insure that casinos will get their fair share of players.

## WILL THE FEDS COME IN?

Prediction is at best a speculative process, particularly the predictions of human behavior. Therefore, what we are about to state may not come to pass—or it may. So, why bother to prognosticate at all? Perhaps for the same reason we spend $350 billion on defense—even if we do not desire a war, we must be prepared to fight.

By the same logic, if we do not want the federal government to regulate the gaming industry, the industry will have to maintain a reputation that is above reproach. And believe us when we say that such regulation is coming—within the next decade, the U.S. government will attempt to control all aspects of public gaming with casino gambling the prime target.

Here are the facts and arguments that support this conclusion:

*1. Gambling in general and casino gaming in particular are already on the upswing in America.*

Currently two states and Puerto Rico have legal casino games while several others allow poker and Blackjack. All but four of the 50 states have some form of legalized gambling.

*2. Gambling is one of the largest businesses in the world in terms of dollar transactions.*

If one measures the handle (amount bet) for both the house and players, annual figures for casino gambling alone would come close to equaling the national defense budget. No industry of this scope can long resist the attention of Congress, especially when that legislative branch is continually looking for more revenue sources to create the "pork barrel" projects that get them re-elected.

*3. Existing casino regulatory agencies have shown a decided favoritism to the industry.*

The latest in this chain of public vs. casino disputes has shown that even when a regulatory body is supposedly constituted to protect the public, it will lean toward protecting its own state revenue instead of arriving at an equitable solution.

*4. The majority of the players are not residents of the state in which they are gambling.*

One can expect little consideration from a state in protecting the residents of another region, except where federal laws are broken (as in the integration of colleges and schools).

*5. Lacking a reasonable solution of their grievances, the public will naturally appeal to a higher authority.*

Although such solutions will not be quickly forthcoming, it is clear that a basically unjust situation must eventually be changed—either peacefully or through some form of revolution. This has been the course of human history. Though the issue we are about to discuss is hardly as momentous as human freedom or democracy, it nevertheless *is* a question of moral imperative.

The issue to which we are referring is the barring of skilled players from gambling casinos which are supposedly open to the public and wherein one supposedly has the opportunity to win as well as to lose. No longer true in New Jersey, barring still takes place in Nevada. Before it was ruled illegal in Atlantic City, there was considerable controversy. Here is a bit of history.

When Atlantic City first opened for casino gambling, it was generally believed that New Jersey law prohibited the barring of skilled players. Operating on that assumption, a number of professional card counters descended upon the Resorts International Casino a few months after it opened. They proceeded to publicly defy the casino personnel, adding insult to injury through public announcements of their winnings. The thoughtless behavior of the professionals brought about a very strong reaction from the casinos, which resulted in Casino Commission Chairman Joseph Lordi allowing the barring of counters.

Ken Uston and others appealed to the Commission, and a series of hearings were held by Commissioner Prospero De Bona. The result of those inquiries was a decision that allowed the casinos to "experiment" with moving the cut card forward of the ¼ to ⅓ dealer mark and shuffling up on suspected card counters.

We have previously remarked upon these so-called "casino countermeasures" and have identified them for what they really are—cheating. Any attempt to alter the random selectivity of the game is clearly an act to change the odds, in this case in favor of the house. Any regulatory body that recommends these kinds of changes is not only a party to cheating the public, but as it was in New Jersey, wholly responsible.

Not knowing or understanding these facts was no excuse. It was apparent to many observers that the activities of the Casino Control Commission were not following the mandate of the electorate, which was to provide an industry that was fair to all.

Is a casino that implements a cheating measure at fault? In the case of New Jersey casinos, the answer is "no." If the state tells the casino to do something, the blame lies with the state. Were the casino to implement such measures—as happens in Nevada—then the fault would lie with casino management. The Nevada Gaming Control Board has carefully avoided serious comment on these measures; but then, the Nevada legislation is slanted in favor of the industry in any public grievance. But, in the case where the regulatory body is supposed to protect the public, the agency should be leaning toward public opinion because the public is in the role of David vs. the Goliaths of the big casinos.

Another mistake of the New Jersey Casino Control Commission was hiring a computer consulting firm to analyze the situation. The Commission erred by failing to choose a firm with proven expertise in the field.

After the 13 days of the so-called experiment, the casinos convinced Lordi to call it off. Casino management claimed a "loss" of $1.4 million—the amount they would have won had the counters not been playing. These figures were based on comparisons between drop and win totals for that period. We argued that measuring a casino's financial standing by the drop is a completely inaccurate method. We illustrated that the drop can be artificially inflated to alter the statistics. This is particularly true when card counters with large bankrolls are playing.

Many card-counting teams reported losses, and at least one dropped its entire bankroll. Our best estimate is that the counters netted $250,000 at most, far less than the reported $1.4 million.

If that's the case, what happened to the rest of the so-called "losers"? The answer to that question lies in understanding the ratio of skilled to unskilled players. It is fair to say that less than 1% of the world's Blackjack players are qualified card counters; of these the gaming commissions have identified less than 100 professionals. So we must again ask the question—why don't the casinos pay more attention to the 99+% instead of the less than 1%? Is it really such a bad thing for a handful of people to win while most players lose? After all, don't businesses write off bad debts and other losses at a much higher rate than the wins of the counters? Doesn't the fact that the game really can be beaten encourage more people to play? If so, shouldn't it be left this way? Doesn't putting an end to the idea of winning do more to hurt the game than to help it? We think that intelligent casino managers and regulators know the answers to these questions. But, somewhere in the ointment is a fly, a cadre of oldtimers who just can't stand to lose. A bright young punk might know more about the game than they do. These people are the ones who cannot see the forest for the trees, yet somehow they convince upper management to go along with them. The results could be disastrous.

The experiment did prove one thing—any extra time spent in shuffling will dramatically lower the house wins. But few people take this into account. Early shuffle-up hurt the house more than the play of the card counters.

By implementing slowdown countermeasures aimed at less than 1% of the players, the house decreases their potential take from the other 99%. If the casino dealt out all the cards, the game would be more fair for the player and more profitable for the house.

We support the following where counters are concerned: When a suspected counter becomes recognized at a casino Blackjack table, the casino personnel should stop the game and award that player a medal (in the manner of the Olympics) to be worn while playing. This medal would entitle a counter to first preference to a seat at the $2 or $5 table; however, that person would be limited to a maximum $10 bet. No one would be barred, and the counter could make a good living of $100 to $150 a day, a drop in the bucket compared to casino revenues. The attendant publicity would actually increase casino revenues far above the relatively small amount lost to the identified professional.

This solution would serve to defuse the current controversy that seems certain to prompt federal intervention. It also might bring back the old conditions favoring casino growth. Casinos in Nevada and New Jersey reported Blackjack winnings of well over $700 million for 1979; reported Blackjack winnings for 1981 were just under $1 billion. In 1983 $1 billion was won in Nevada alone.

That's not too shabby a business. Regulatory agencies and casinos would be wise not to kill the golden goose.

# CHAPTER SEVENTEEN

# PROPOSED INTERNATIONAL RULES FOR BLACKJACK

## by STANLEY ROBERTS

In a decade and a half from 1963 to 1978, we have witnessed a remarkable growth in the gaming industry. The total gross revenue (for Blackjack alone) jumped over 66% EACH YEAR. On the other hand, the total increase in other table games was slightly over 50% EACH YEAR.

The real growth in casino revenue has not come about because of entertainment policy or because of increased advertising by the casinos; it has come about because of player interest in the game of Blackjack. More and more people have come to believe that they have a good shot at winning at the Blackjack table, and so they're willing to take a risk at playing the game.

Well, then, who or what is responsible for this growth in casino revenue? The people who have written and publicized books showing that Blackjack can be beaten. And, these people are my co-authors of this book.

We are fortunate that there is now more than one casino gaming control body in the United States. To be specific, there are two: New Jersey's Casino Control Commission and the Nevada Gaming Control Board. Although New Jersey is certainly the newer and less experienced of these bodies, in my opinion, New Jersey has now taken the leadership position. This is particularly true because the New Jersey Commission has oriented itself toward some measure of consumer protection while the Nevada Gaming Control Board has shown very little interest in the consumer. Their mandate is to protect the industry.

In these days of national consumer interest, I think that it's time for Nevada to reevaluate its policy. The fact that there is more than one gaming authority is going to create competition and that is good for the public and it is, in fact, the American way. I also believe that this will be good for the industry. There is something about competition that has always yielded a better product and a better business for all those people who were involved in it.

We have stated many times that the Nevada Gaming Control Board has done an exemplary job in policing the industry, in spite of the fact that they have a rather small staff. On the other hand, that does not mean they have done a perfect job and that does not mean the job cannot be improved—indeed, we believe it needs to be.

One of the first things these state agencies need to do is take control of the industry. They must do this without regard to any influence that may be exerted upon them by casino ownership. These agencies are in a sense referees between the player and the casino.

There are three areas in which both of these agencies must take action. When dealing the game of Blackjack, regardless of the number of decks used (one, two, four, six, or eight decks), the casino MUST deal EVERY card out of the deck. Any other pattern of early shuffle-up, cutting off of cards (which actually has no effect), or placing a cut card somewhere prior to the end of the deck is a violation of the principle of random selectivity.

The second area is the barring of counters in Nevada. If you are going to deal a game to the public, then you cannot selectively decide which portion of the public you want to deal to. The fact of the matter is that only one person in a thousand or less has the ability to beat the game. That person will not take that large a sum of money out of the casino because even he is only working with a small edge. Therefore, the casino should be content to get its share from the losers and not persecute the winners. Some casino managers do not feel that another person has the right to use their casino as a place to make a living. Those people do not understand that the gaming business operates in a particular way and they cannot seek to change the rules arbitrarily to make it more beneficial for them. It is our best estimate that the total amount of money won by counters in casinos does not even equal 2% of the gross win. Furthermore, it obviously hasn't affected the trend of things in a negative way. So, one can only assume that having counters in the casino who win occasionally is good for the overall picture.

Last, and most important, it is time to standardize the rules for Blackjack and they should be standardized in an international way so that all casinos around the world will deal the game in the proper manner.

Following are the rules we propose for international Blackjack play:

1. One, two, or four decks (dealt from a shoe) may be used. When a shoe is used, it must be inspected by the Gaming Control Board and carry a visible seal of approval.

2. The dealer will shuffle the cards thoroughly and offer a cut to one of the players. The deck must be cut. If all players decline, the dealer will cut the deck.

3. All cards must be put into play from the deck(s) used.

4. The first card will be burned, but first it must be exposed for the players to see.

5. All players' cards will be dealt face up. Players may not handle the cards. All signals for play will be given by hand.

6. A change of dealers cannot be made until the deck has been exhausted and is ready to be shuffled.

7. When the table is idle, all cards will be spread out, face up.

8. The dealer must hit all 16's and stand on all 17's, including

soft 17's. Players' Blackjack pays 3 to 2.

9. Any pair may be split and played as a separate hand with an equal bet. Up to three additional hands may be split from an original hand. All ten-value cards are considered pairs. All split pairs are played individually, including aces.

10. Doubling down will be permitted on any combination of the first two cards. Since a split hand is a new hand, it may be doubled on.

11. Any two-card hand, including previously split hands may be surrendered giving up half the original bet, unless the dealer has a natural.

12. Insurance will be offered on all dealer's ace up-cards, up to half the original bet, paying at 2 to 1. Dealer's hole card must be taken immediately.

13. Any player may play as many hands as are vacant and adjacent to his original hand without penalty, minimum, or reservation. When the casino is crowded, the house may declare a one-hand maximum limit.

14. The house may determine the table limits but there must be at least a two-hundred-unit difference between minimum and maximum bets.

15. No player may bet more than ten times the previous amount wagered on all hands played in the last round, including all splits, doubles, and insurance.

Since casinos have been making Blackjack more and more unfavorable for players, they are beginning to lose interest in it. Only a better game will bring back the big players. Without a change in the rules, Blackjack will go the way that faro has gone and the way that roulette is heading—a dying pastime that has become unprofitable for both the player and the house.

These are our suggestions for consideration by the Gaming Control Board of Nevada and the Casino Control Commission of New Jersey. Below you will find their addresses. I strongly recommend that each of you who has an interest in the game of Blackjack write to these bodies, letting them know that you care about these items and that you want to see them implemented. If they receive a reasonable volume of mail, they will be forced to consider these matters seriously and to act on them. If they don't receive any mail, the conditions will continue to exist and they will be to the detriment of not only you, the player, but of the industry as well.

State of Nevada
Gaming Control Board
1150 East William Street
Carson City, Nevada 89710

State of New Jersey
Casino Control Commission
379 West State Street
Trenton, New Jersey 08625

# APPENDIX A

## BASIC STRATEGY FOR SINGLE DECK
## RENO-LAKE TAHOE RULES

### PAIR SPLITTING STRATEGY

| DEALER SHOWS | YOUR HAND |
|---|---|
| 3–7 | (2,2) |
| 4–7 | (3,3) |
| Never | (4,4) |
| Never | (5,5) |
| 2–6 | (6,6) |
| 2–7 | (7,7) |
| Always | (8,8) |
| 2–9 (Except 7) | (9,9) |
| Never | (10,10) |
| Always | (Ace, Ace) |

### HARD DOUBLING STRATEGY

| DEALER SHOWS | YOUR HAND |
|---|---|
| 2–9 | 10 |
| Always | 11 |

DOUBLE AFTER SPLIT NOT ALLOWED
DEALER HITS SOFT 17

## BASIC STRATEGY FOR SINGLE DECK
## RENO-LAKE TAHOE RULES (con't)

### SOFT STANDING STRATEGY

| YOU STAND ON | DEALER SHOWS |
|---|---|
| 18 | 2–8 |
| 19 | 9 or 10 |
| 19 | Ace |

### HARD STANDING STRATEGY

| YOU STAND ON | DEALER SHOWS |
|---|---|
| 13 | 2 or 3 |
| 12 | 4–6 |
| 17 | 7,8, or Ace |
| 17 | 9 |
| 17 or (7,7) | 10 |

DOUBLE AFTER SPLIT NOT ALLOWED
DEALER HITS SOFT 17

## BASIC STRATEGY FOR DOUBLE DECK

### SURRENDER STRATEGY

| DEALER SHOWS | YOUR HAND |
|---|---|
| Ace | (10,6) or (9,7) |
| 10 | (10,6), (10,5) |
| | (9,7) or (9,6) |

### PAIR SPLITTING STRATEGY

| YOUR HAND | DEALER SHOWS |
|---|---|
| (2,2) | 4–7 (*2–7) |
| (3,3) | 4–7 (*2–7) |
| (4,4) | Never (*5 or 6) |
| (5,5) | Never |
| (6,6) | 3–6, (*2–6) |
| (7,7) | 2–7 |
| (8,8) | Always |
| (9,9) | 2–9 (Except 7) |
| (10,10) | Never |
| (Ace, Ace) | Always |

DOUBLE AFTER SPLIT NOT ALLOWED
(*DOUBLE AFTER SPLIT ALLOWED)

## BASIC STRATEGY FOR DOUBLE DECK (con't)

### SOFT DOUBLING STRATEGY

| YOUR HAND | DEALER SHOWS |
|---|---|
| (Ace, 2) or (Ace, 3) | 5 or 6 |
| (Ace, 4) or (Ace, 5) | 4–6 |
| (Ace, 6) | 3–6 |
| (Ace, 7) | 3–6 |
| (Ace, 8) | Never |
| (Ace, 9) | Never |

### HARD DOUBLING STRATEGY

| YOUR HAND | DEALER SHOWS |
|---|---|
| 8 | Never |
| 9 | 2–6 |
| 10 | 2–9 |
| (9,2) or (8,3) | 2–10 |
| (7,4) or (6,5) | Always |

DOUBLE AFTER SPLIT NOT ALLOWED
(*DOUBLE AFTER SPLIT ALLOWED)

## BASIC STRATEGY FOR DOUBLE DECK (con't)

### SOFT STANDING STRATEGY

| DEALER SHOWS | YOU STAND ON |
|---|---|
| 2–8 | 18 |
| 9 or 10 | 19 |
| Ace | 19 |

### HARD STANDING STRATEGY

| DEALER SHOWS | YOU STAND ON |
|---|---|
| 2 or 3 | 13 |
| 4–6 | 12 |
| 7,8, or Ace | 17 |
| 9 | 17 |
| 10 | 17 |

DOUBLE AFTER SPLIT NOT ALLOWED
(*DOUBLE AFTER SPLIT ALLOWED)

# BASIC STRATEGY FOR FOUR OR MORE DECKS

## SURRENDER STRATEGY

| DEALER SHOWS | YOUR HAND |
|---|---|
| Ace | (10,6) or (9,7) |
| 10 | (10,6), (10,5) |
| | (9,7), or (9,6) |
| 9 | (10,6) or (9,7) |

## PAIR SPLITTING STRATEGY

| YOUR HAND | DEALER SHOWS |
|---|---|
| (2,2) | 4-7 (*2-7) |
| (3,3) | 4-7 (*2-7) |
| (4,4) | Never (*5 or 6) |
| (5,5) | Never |
| (6,6) | 3-6 (*2-6) |
| (7,7) | 2-7 |
| (8,8) | Always |
| (9,9) | 2-9 (Except 7) |
| (10,10) | Never |
| (Ace, Ace) | Always |

DOUBLE AFTER SPLIT NOT ALLOWED
(*DOUBLE AFTER SPLIT ALLOWED)

## BASIC STRATEGY FOR FOUR
## OR MORE DECKS (con't)

### SOFT DOUBLING STRATEGY

| YOUR HAND | DEALER SHOWS |
|---|---|
| (Ace, 2) or (Ace, 3) | 5 or 6 |
| (Ace, 4) or (Ace, 5) | 4-6 |
| (Ace, 6) | 3-6 |
| (Ace, 7) | 3-6 |
| (Ace, 8) | Never |
| (Ace, 9) | Never |

### HARD DOUBLING STRATEGY

| YOUR HAND | DEALER SHOWS |
|---|---|
| 8 | Never |
| 9 | 3-6 |
| 10 | 2-9 |
| 11 | 2-10 |

DOUBLE AFTER SPLIT NOT ALLOWED
(*DOUBLE AFTER SPLIT ALLOWED)

## BASIC STRATEGY FOR FOUR
## OR MORE DECKS (con't)

### SOFT STANDING STRATEGY

| DEALER SHOWS | YOU STAND ON |
| --- | --- |
| 2–8 | 18 |
| 9 or 10 | 19 |
| Ace | 19 |

### HARD STANDING STRATEGY

| DEALER SHOWS | YOU STAND ON |
| --- | --- |
| 2 or 3 | 13 |
| 4–6 | 12 |
| 7, 8, or Ace | 17 |
| 9 | 17 |
| 10 | 17 |

DOUBLE AFTER SPLIT NOT ALLOWED
(*DOUBLE AFTER SPLIT ALLOWED)

## BASIC STRATEGY FOR FOUR OR MORE DECKS
### (WITH SINGLE DECK₁ AND DOUBLE DECK₂ EXCEPTIONS, AS NOTED)

### SURRENDER STRATEGY

| DEALER SHOWS | YOUR HAND |
|---|---|
| Ace | (10,6) or (9,7) |
| Ace[1] | (10,6) (Except 9,7) |
| 10 | (10,6), (10,5) |
| | (9,7), or (9,6) |
| 10[1] | +(7,7) |
| 9 | (10,6) or (9,7) |
| 9[1,2] | (Except 10,6 or 9,7) |

### PAIR SPLITTING STRATEGY

| YOUR HAND | DEALER SHOWS |
|---|---|
| (2,2) | 4–7 (*2–7) |
| (2,2)[1] | 3–7 (*2–7) |
| (3,3) | 4–7 (*2–7) |
| (4,4) | Never (*5 or 6) |
| (4,4)[1] | Never (*4–6) |
| (5,5) | Never |
| (6,6) | 3–6 (*2–6) |
| (6,6)[1] | 2–6 (*2–7) |
| (7,7) | 2–7 |
| (7,7)[1] | 2–7 (*2–8) |
| (8,8) | Always |
| (9,9) | 2–9 (Except 7) |
| (10,10) | Never |
| (Ace, Ace) | Always |

DOUBLE AFTER SPLIT NOT ALLOWED
(*DOUBLE AFTER SPLIT ALLOWED)
DEALER STANDS ON SOFT 17
(**DEALER HITS SOFT 17)

# BASIC STRATEGY FOR FOUR OR MORE DECKS (WITH SINGLE DECK₁ AND DOUBLE DECK₂ EXCEPTIONS, AS NOTED) (con't)

## SOFT DOUBLING STRATEGY

| YOUR HAND | DEALER SHOWS |
|---|---|
| (Ace, 2) or (Ace, 3) | 5 or 6 |
| (Ace, 2)₁ or (Ace, 3)₁ | 4–6 |
| (Ace, 4) or (Ace, 5) | 4–6 |
| (Ace, 6) | 3–6 |
| (Ace, 6)₁ | 2–6 |
| (Ace, 7) | 3–6 |
| (Ace, 8) | Never |
| (Ace, 8)₁ | 6 |
| (Ace, 9) | Never |

## HARD DOUBLING STRATEGY

| YOUR HAND | DEALER SHOWS |
|---|---|
| 8 | Never |
| (5,3)₁ or (4,4)₁ | 5 or 6 |
| (6,2)₁ | Never |
| 9 | 3–6 |
| 9₁,₂ | 2–6 |
| 10 | 2–9 |
| 11 | 2–10 |
| 11₁,₂ | Always |
| (9,2)₂ or (8,3)₂ | 2–10 |
| (7,4)₂ or (6,5)₂ | Always |

DOUBLE AFTER SPLIT NOT ALLOWED
(*DOUBLE AFTER SPLIT ALLOWED)
DEALER STANDS ON SOFT 17
(**DEALER HITS SOFT 17)

## BASIC STRATEGY FOR FOUR OR MORE DECKS
## (WITH SINGLE DECK$_1$ AND DOUBLE DECK$_2$
## EXCEPTIONS, AS NOTED) (con't)

### SOFT STANDING STRATEGY

| DEALER SHOWS | YOU STAND ON |
|---|---|
| 2–8 | 18 |
| 9 or 10 | 19 |
| Ace | 19 |
| Ace$_1$ | 18 (**19) |

### HARD STANDING STRATEGY

| DEALER SHOWS | YOU STAND ON |
|---|---|
| 2 or 3 | 13 |
| 4–6 | 12 |
| 7,8, or Ace | 17 |
| 9 | 17 |
| 10 | 17 |
| 10$_1$ | +(7,7) |

DOUBLE AFTER SPLIT NOT ALLOWED
(*DOUBLE AFTER SPLIT ALLOWED)
DEALER STANDS ON SOFT 17
(**DEALER HITS SOFT 17)

# BASIC STRATEGY FOR FOUR OR MORE DECKS ATLANTIC CITY RULES

## SURRENDER STRATEGY*

| DEALER SHOWS | YOUR HAND |
|---|---|
| Ace | 5–7 and 12–17 |
| 10 | 14–16 |
| 9 | (10,6) or (9,7) |

## PAIR SPLITTING STRATEGY

| YOUR HAND | DEALER SHOWS |
|---|---|
| (2,2) | 2–7 |
| (3,3) | 2–7 |
| (4,4) | 5 or 6 |
| (5,5) | Never |
| (6,6) | 2–6 |
| (7,7) | 2–7 |
| (8,8) | Always |
| (9,9) | 2–9, Except 7 |
| (10,10) | Never |
| (Ace, Ace) | Always |

*In May, 1981, Atlantic City canceled the Surrender option. If Surrender is not reinstated, use Basic Strategy for Las Vegas 4 Decks, DASA, without Surrender.*

## BASIC STRATEGY FOR FOUR OR MORE DECKS
## ATLANTIC CITY RULES (con't)

### SOFT DOUBLING STRATEGY

| YOUR HAND | DEALER SHOWS |
|---|---|
| (Ace, 2) or (Ace, 3) | 5 or 6 |
| (Ace, 4) or (Ace, 5) | 4–6 |
| (Ace, 6) | 3–6 |
| (Ace, 7) | 3–6 |
| (Ace, 8) | Never |
| (Ace, 9) | Never |

### HARD DOUBLING STRATEGY

| YOUR HAND | DEALER SHOWS |
|---|---|
| 8 | Never |
| 9 | 3–6 |
| 10 | 2–9 |
| 11 | 2–10 |

# BASIC STRATEGY FOR FOUR OR MORE DECKS
## ATLANTIC CITY RULES (con't)

## SOFT STANDING STRATEGY

| DEALER SHOWS | YOU STAND ON |
| --- | --- |
| 2–8 | 18 |
| 9 or 10 | 19 |
| Ace | 19 |

## HARD STANDING STRATEGY

| DEALER SHOWS | YOU STAND ON |
| --- | --- |
| 2 or 3 | 13 |
| 4–6 | 12 |
| 7,8 or Ace | 17 |
| 9 | 17 |
| 10 | 17 |

## KEEPING YOUR GAMING KNOWLEDGE CURRENT THROUGH *WIN*

Now that you are well on your way to becoming a proficient Blackjack player, you will want to keep abreast of all the latest rule variations in the game in casinos around the world. *WIN* Magazine (formerly *Gambling Times)* can give you that information.

Since February of 1977, readers of *WIN* Magazine (formerly *Gambling Times)* have profited immensely. They have done so by using the information they have read each month. if that sounds like a simple solution to winning more and losing less, well it is! Readers look to *WIN* for that very specific reason. And it delivers.

*WIN* is totally dedicated to showing readers how to win more money in every form of legalized gambling. How much you're going to win depends on many factors, but it's going to be considerably more than the cost of a subscription.

## WINNING AND MONEY

Winning, that's what *WIN* is all about. And money, that's what *WIN* it all about. Because winning and money go hand in hand.

Here's what the late Vince Lombardi, the famous football coach of the Green Bay Packers, had to say about winning:

"It's not a sometime thing. Winning is a habit. There

is no room for second place. There is only one place in my game and that is first place. I have finished second twice in my time at Green Bay and I don't ever want to finish second again. The objective is to win—fairly, squarely, decently, by the rules—but to win. To beat the other guy. maybe that sounds hard or cruel. I don't think it is. It is and has always been an American Zeal to be first in anything we do, and to win, and to win and to win."

Mr. Lombardi firmly believed that being a winner is "man's finest hour." *WIN* believes it is too, while being a loser is depressing, ego-deflating, expensive and usually very lonely. "Everybody loves a winner" may be a cliche, but it's true. Winners command respect and are greatly admired. Winners are also very popular and have an abundance of friends. You may have seen a winner in a casino, with a bevy of girls surrounding him...or remember one who could get just about any girl he wanted.

Some of the greatest gamblers in the world also have strong views on what winning is all about. Here's what two of them have to say on the subject:

"To be a winner, a man has to feel good about himself and know he has some kind of advantage going in. I never made bets on even chances. Smart is better than lucky."
— "Titanic" Thompson

"When it comes to winnin', I got me a one-track mind. You gotta want to win more than anything else. And you gotta have confidence. You can't pretend to have it. That's no good. You gotta have it. You gotta know. Guessers are losers. Gamblin's just as simple as that."
—Johnny Moss

*WIN* will bring you the knowledge you need to come home a winner and come home in the money. For it is knowledge, the kind of knowledge you'll get in its pages, that separates winners from losers. It's winning and money that *WIN* offers you. *WIN* will be your working manual to winning wealth.

The current distribution of this magazine is limited to selected newsstands in selected cities. Additionally, at newstands where it is available, it's being snapped up, as soon as it's displayed, by gamblers who know a sure bet when they see one.

So if you're serious about winning, you're best off subscribing to *WIN*. Then you can always count on its being there, conveniently delivered to your mailbox—and what's more, it will be there one to two weeks before it appears on the newsstands. You'll be among the first to receive the current issue as soon as it comes off the presses, and being first is the way to be a winner.

Having every monthly issue of *WIN* will enable you to build an "Encyclopedia of Gambling," since the contents of this magazine are full of sound advice that will be as good in five or ten years as it is now.

As you can see, a subscription to *WIN* is your best bet for a future of knowledgeable gambling. It's your ticket to *WINNING* and *MONEY*.

Take the time to read the following offer. As you can see, *WIN* has gone all out to give you outstanding bonuses. You can join the knowledgeable players who have learned that *WIN* helps them to win more money.

# NINE NEW WAYS TO GET 12 WINNING ISSUES OF *WIN* FREE...

Every month over 250,000 readers trust *WIN* to introduce powerful new winning strategies and systems. Using proven scientific methods, the world's leading experts show you how to win big money in the complex field of gambling.

*WIN* has shown how progressive slot machines can be beaten. Readers have discovered important new edges in blackjack. They've been shown how to know for sure when an opponent is bluffing at poker. *WIN* has also spelled out winning methods for football, baseball and basketball. They've published profound new ways of beating horses. Their team of experts will uncover information in the months ahead that's certain to be worth thousands of dollars to you.

In fact, the features are so revolutionary that they must take special precautions to make sure *WIN* readers learn these secrets long before anyone else. So how much is *WIN* worth to you? Well...

NOW *WIN* CAN BE BETTER THAN FREE! Here's how: This BONUS package comes AUTOMATICALLY TO YOU WHEN YOU SUBSCRIBE...or goes to a friend if you give a gift subscription.

★1.  A CARD that entitles you to a 50% discount at over 2,000 quality hotels in over 400 cities, mainly in North America and the Caribbean. Only the finest hotels are included; chains such as Holiday Inn, Sheraton, Hilton, Best Western, Marriott and Ramada Inns. Discounts are good 365 days per year. Stay as long as you like, subject to availability. Save as much as $100 per night.

★2.  A 50% discount on a one week stay in over 2,000 condominiums, worldwide, including the United States, Canada, Mexico, France, Bahamas, Jamaica, Italy, Spain, Germany, Austria, Aruba and many more! Reservations made by a toll free number.

★3.  Free Kodak film for life when you use our specified National Processing laboratory, which gives a 40% discount off Kodak list prices for developing. Free Kodak Color film, any size, speed or exposure to fit your camera, is provided with each roll of film developed.

★4.  A 5% REBATE on the lowest available scheduled Airline fares in the US and up to a 45% REBATE on international flights when you book through our contract agency, San Diego Travel. Licensed and Bonded since 1963. Reservations can be made by a toll free number.

★5.  A 3 day/2 night FREE vacation for two in your choice of Las Vegas, Reno, Tahoe, Atlantic City or Hawaii, plus Disneyland or DisneyWorld—when you book your air fare and reservations through our travel agency, San Diego Travel.

★6.  A funpack booklet entitling the holder to over $250 in discounts at local businesses in your choice of: Las Vegas, Reno, Tahoe, Atlantic City, Hawaii, Orlando, Carlsbad-Oceanside, Disneyland, Palm Springs or Acapulco, Mexico. Includes cash, meals, chips, Keno, lucky bucks, slot tokens, drinks, entertainment, attractions and much, much more! Outside of Nevada the funpack may not include cash or gambling benefits. Good 7 days a week, including all holidays.

★7.   15% to 50% discounts on over 1,000 cruise trips. Savings can be as much as $1,000 per cruise. Includes a $50 per cabin bar-boutique ship credit. Reservations by toll free number.

★8.   A standard discount on car rental from Hertz, Avis, Budget and Alamo car rental agencies. Guaranteed lowest prices, not available to the public. Toll free numbers in US & Canada.

★9.   Your choice of a FREE 3-piece, 6-piece or all 9-piece set of English Leather Designer Luggage. Total value of all 9 pieces is $199.90. Gift certificate with each subscription.

To begin your delivery of *WIN* magazine at once, enclose a payment of $36.00 by check or money order (U.S. currency), Mastercard or Visa. Add $5.00 per year for postage outside the United States. Send payment to:

> *WIN* MAGAZINE
> 16760 Stagg St., Suite 213
> Van Nuys, CA 91406-1642

# Other Valuable Sources of Knowledge Available Through *Gambling Times Inc.*

*Here are some additional sources you can turn to for worthwhile gambling information:*

*The Experts Blackjack Newsletter.*
This bi-monthly newsletter has all the top blackjack Experts working just for you. Features answers, strategies and insights that were never before possible. Yearly subscriptions are $30 for 6 issues.

# OTHER BOOKS AVAILABLE

If you can't find the following books at your local bookstore, they may be ordered directly from *Gambling Times*, 16760 Stagg St., Van Nuys, CA 91406. Information on how to order is on page 227.

## *Blackjack Books*

**The Beginner's Guide to Winning Blackjack** by Stanley Roberts—The world's leading blackjack writer shows beginners to the game how to obtain an instant advantage through the simplest of techniques. Covering Basic Strategy for all major casino areas from Las Vegas to the Bahamas, Atlantic City and Reno/Tahoe, Roberts provides a simple system to immediately know when the remaining cards favor the player. The entire method can be learned in less than two hours and taken to the casinos to produce sure profits.
Softbound. $10.00. (ISBN: 0-89746-014-6)

**Million Dollar Blackjack** by Ken Uston—Every blackjack enthusiast or gaming traveler who fancies himself a "21" player can improve his game with this explosive bestseller. Ken Uston shows you how he and his team won over 4 million dollars at blackjack. Now, for the first time, you can find out how he did it and how his system can help you. Includes playing and betting strategies, winning secrets, protection from cheaters, Uston's Advanced Point Count System, and a glossary of inside terms used by professionals.
Softbound. $14.95. (ISBN: 0-914314-08-4)

**Winning Blackjack** by Stanley Roberts—It is the simplest, most accurate blackjack system ever devised. The average person takes about eight hours both to read the system completely and master it. It does not require a photographic memory. All you really have to do is pay attention to the game. Businessmen and housewives alike report consistent winnings of up to $500 a day when using this system. This manual is complete in every way. It not only tells

you how to play, it also tells you where to play, how much to bet and some very important tips about the art of casino play. There is a special section for beating multi-deck games and everything you need to know about blackjack in Las Vegas, Reno, Tahoe, Atlantic City and a host of other casino resorts around the world. This book has the power to completely transform you life! *Winning Blackjack* is large, 8½" × 11", and includes pull-apart flash cards printed on card stock.
Softbound. $95.00. (ISBN: 0-914314-00-9)

## Poker Books

**According to Doyle** by Doyle Brunson—Acknowledged by most people as the world's best all-around poker player, twice World Champion Doyle Brunson brings you his homespun wisdom from over 30 years as a professional poker player. This book will not only show you how to win at poker, it will give you valuable insights into how to better handle that poker game called LIFE.
Softbound. $6.95. (ISBN: 0-89746-003-0)

**Caro on Gambling** by Mike Caro—The world's leading poker writer covers all the aspects of gambling from his regular columns in *Gambling Times* magazine and *Poker Player* newspaper. Discussing odds and probabilities, bluffing and raising, psychology and character, this book will bring to light valuable concepts that can be turned into instant profits in home games as well as in the poker palaces of the West.
Softbound. $6.95. (ISBN: 0-89746-029-4)

**Caro's Book of Tells** by Mike Caro—The photographic body language of poker. Approximately 180 photographs with text explaining when a player is bluffing, when he's got the winning hand—and WHY. Based on accurate investigation; it is NOT guesswork. Even the greatest of gamblers has some giveaway behavior. For the first time in print, one of the world's top poker players reveals how he virtually can read minds because nearly every player has a "tell." Seal the leaks in your poker game and empty your opponent's chip tray.
Hardbound. $20.00. (ISBN: 0-914314-04-1)

**Free Money: How to Win in the Cardrooms of California** by Michael Wiesenberg—Computer expert and poker writer par excellence, Michael Wiesenberg delivers critical knowledge to those who play in the poker rooms of the western states. Wiesenberg gives you the precise meaning of the rules as well as the mathematics of poker to aid public and private poker players alike. Wiesenberg, a prolific author, is published by more gaming periodicals than any other writer.
Softbound. $8.95. (ISBN: 0-89746-027-8)

**New Poker Games** by Mike Caro—In this ground-breaking book, you'll learn Mad Genius Mike Caro's new ways to play an old game. Some of the games are Caro originals, while others are contributed by readers of *WIN* Magazine. Loaded with descriptions and winning strategies for novel forms of poker. Caro is recognized as the leading poker teacher of the Nineties!
Softbound. $5.95. (ISBN: 0-89746-040-5)

**Poker for Women** by Mike Caro—How women can take advantage of the special male-female ego wars at the poker table and win. This book also has non-poker everyday value for women. Men can be destroyed at the poker table by coy, cunning or aggressive women. That's because, on a subconscious level, men expect women to act traditionally. This book tells women when to flirt, when to be tough and when to whimper. Many of the tactics are tried and proven by Caro's own students. This book does not claim that women are better players, merely that there are strategies available to them that are not available to their male opponents.
Softbound. $6.95. (ISBN: 0-89746-009-X)

**The Railbird** by Rex Jones—The ultimate kibitzer, the man who watches from the rail in the poker room, has unique insights into the character and performance of all poker players. From this vantage point, Rex Jones, Ph.D., blends his expertise and considerable education in anthropology with his lifetime of poker playing and watching. The result is a delightful book with exceptional values for those who want to avoid the fatal errors of bad players and capitalize upon the qualities that make up the winning strengths of outstanding poker players.
Softbound. $6.95. (ISBN: 0-89746-028-6)

**Tales Out of Tulsa** by Bobby Baldwin—Oklahoma-born Bobby Baldwin, the youngest player to ever win the World Championship of Poker, is considered to be among the top five poker players in the world. Known affectionately as "The Owl," this brilliant poker genius, wise beyond his years, brings the benefits of his experience to the pages of this book.
Softbound. $6.95 (ISBN: 0-89746-006-5)

**Wins, Places, and Pros** by Tex Sheahan—With more than 50 years of experience as a professional poker player and cardroom manager/tournament director, Tex lets his readers in on the secrets that separate the men from the boys at the poker table. Descriptions of poker events, playing experiences from all over the world, and those special personalities who are the masters of the game. . .Tex knows them all and lays it out in his marvelous easy-to-read style.
Softbound. $6.95. (ISBN: 0-89746-008-1)

## *Casino Games*

**The Gambling Times Guide to Casino Games** by Len Miller—The co-founder of *Gambling Times* magazine vividly describes the casino games and explains their rules and betting procedures. This easy-to-follow guide covers blackjack, craps, roulette, keno, video machines, progressive slots and more. After reading this book, you'll play like a pro!
Softbound. $9.95. (ISBN: 0-89746-017-0)

**The Gambling Times Guide to Craps** by N.B. Winkless, Jr.—The ultimate craps book for beginners and experts alike. It provides you with a program to tackle the house edge that can be used on a home computer. This text shows you which bets to avoid and tells you the difference between craps in Nevada and craps in other gaming resort areas. It includes a glossary of terms and a directory of dealer schools.
Softbound. $9.95. (ISBN: 0-89746-013-8)

**How to Win at Casino Gaming Tournaments** by Haven E. Haley— Win your share of the millions of dollars and fabulous prizes being awarded to gaming contestants, and have the glory of being a World Champion. Poker, gin rummy, backgammon, craps, blackjack and baccarat are all popular tournament games. The rules, special tournament regulations, playing procedures, and how to obtain free entry are fully explained in this informative manual. The tournament promoters—who they are, where they hold events—and the cash and prizes awarded are explained in detail. Tournament play usually requires special strategy changes, which are detailed in this book.

Softbound. $8.95. (ISBN: 0-89746-016-2)

## General Interest Books

**Gambling and the Law** by I. Nelson Rose—The definitive work on the subject of law as it relates to the world of gaming. Professor Rose explains all facets of gambling law and how they apply to players, professionals and casino owners and employees. A MUST read for anyone concerned with gambling. Topics addressed include: Taking gambling losses and expenses off your taxes; How to avoid paying gambling debts; What to do if cheated; The legality of home poker; Your rights in the casino; Getting a gaming license and Suing to get your losses back. Destined to be the most influential gambling book of the decade.
Hardbound. $19.95 (ISBN: 0-89746X-066-9)

**GT Guide to Bingo** by Roger Snowden—Gives bingo history, instructs on how to best play the game, describes over 108 variations and explain how you can increase your chances of winning by selecting the right locations to play. The author is an editor of the *Bingo Bugle* newspaper.
Softbound. $6.95. (ISBN: 0-89746-057-X)

**GT Guide to European and Asian Games** by Syd Helprin—A comprehensive guide to casino gambling in faraway lands. Covers such games as: Australian mini dice, *trente et quarante, banca francesa, punto banco, pai gow, kalooke, sic bo, fan tan* and many others.

Important information for the informed gambler.
Softbound. $7.95 (ISBN: 0-89746-062-6)

**The Gambling Times Guide to Systems That Win, Volume I and Volume II**—For those who want to broaden their gambling knowledge, this two-volume set offers complete gambling systems used by the experts. Learn their strategies and how to incorporate them into your gambling style. **Volume I** covers 12 systems that win for roulette, craps, backgammon, slot machines, horse racing, baseball, basketball and football.
Softbound. $5.95. (ISBN: 0-89746-034-0)
**Volume II** features 12 more systems that win, covering horse racing, craps, blackjack, slot machines, jai alai and baseball.
Softbound. $5.95. (ISBN: 0-89746-034-0)

The Gambling Times Guide to Winning Systems, Volume II—
For those who take their gambling seriously, *Gambling Times* presents a set of proven winning systems. Learn how the experts beat the house edge and become consistent winners. **Volume II** contains 12 winning systems covering poker bluffing, pitching analysis, greyhound handicapping and roulette.
Softbound. $5.95. (ISBN: 0-89746-033-2)

**Gambling Times Presents Winning Systems and Methods, Volume I and Volume II**—This two-volume collection of winning strategies by some of the nation's leading experts on gambling will help you in your quest to beat the percentages. **Volume I** includes several chapters on blackjack, as well as methods for beating baseball, basketball, hockey, steeplechase and grass racing.
Softbound. $5.95. (ISBN: 0-89746-036-7)
**Volume II** contains an analysis of keno and video poker, as well as systems for success in sports betting and horse racing.
Softbound. $5.95. (ISBN: 0-89746-037-5)

**The Gambling Times Quiz Book** by Mike Caro—Learn while testing your knowledge. Caro's book includes questions and answers on the concepts and information published in previous issues of *Gambling Times*. Caro

tells why an answer is correct and credit is given to the author whose *Gambling Times* article suggested the question. This book covers only established fact, not the personal opinions of authors, and Caro's inimitable style makes this an easy-reading, easy-learning book.
Softbound. $5.95. (ISBN: 0-89746-031-6)

**Golf, Gambling and Gamesmanship** by Gary Moore—After three decades as a golf course hustler, the author embarked on a six-year search to find winning systems for gambling on golf. The results are presented here. Read this book and dominate your buddies all the way to the 19th hole!
Softbound. $7.95 (ISBN: 0-89746-054-5)

**The Mathematics of Gambling** by Edward O. Thorp—The "Albert Einstein of gambling" presents his second book on the subject. His first book, *Beat The Dealer,* set the gambling world on its heels and struck fear into the cold-blooded hearts of Las Vegas casino-owners in 1962. Now, more than twenty years later, Dr. Thorp again challenges the odds by bringing out a simple to understand version of more than thirty years of exploration into all aspects of what separates winners from losers. . . knowing the real meaning of the parameters of the games.
Softbound. $7.95. (ISBN: 0-89746-019-7)

**P$yching Out Vegas** by Marvin Karlins, Ph.D.—The dream merchants who build and operate gaming resorts subtly work on the casino patron to direct his attention, control his actions and turn his pockets inside out. At last, their techniques are revealed to you by a noted psychologist who shows you how you can successfully control your behavior and turn a losing attitude into a lifetime winning streak.
Hardbound. $14.95. (ISBN: 0-914314-03-3)

**Winning by Computer** by Dr. Donald Sullivan—Now, for the first time, the wonders of computer technology are harnessed for the gambler. Dr. Sullivan explains how to figure the odds and identify key factors in all forms of race and sports handicapping.
Softbound. $5.95. (ISBN: 0-89746-018-9)

# *Sports Betting Books*

**The Gambling Times Guide to Basketball Handicapping** by Barbara Nathan—This easy-to-read, highly informative book is the definitive guide to basketball betting. Expert sports handicapper Barbara Nathan provides handicapping knowledge, insightful coverage, and step-by-step guidance for money management. The advantages and disadvantages of relying on sports services are also covered. Softbound. $5.95. (ISBN: 0-89746-023-5)

**The Gambling Times Guide to Football Handicapping** by Bob McCune—Starting with the novice's approach to handicapping football, and winding up with some of the more sophisticated team selection techniques in the sports handicapping realm, this book will actually tell the reader how to forecast, *in advance,* the final scores of most major national football games. The author's background and expertise on the subject will put money into any sports gambler's pocket. Softbound. $5.95. (ISBN: 0-89746-022-7)

**The Gambling Times Guide to Greyhound Racing** by William E. McBride—This complete discussion of greyhound racing is a must for anyone who is just beginning to appreciate this exciting and profitable sport. The book begins with a brief overview detailing the origins of greyhound racing and pari-mutuel betting, and explains the greyhound track environment, betting procedures, and handicapping methods. Includes an appendix of various greyhound organizations, a review of greyhound books, and an interesting section on famous dogs and personalities in the world of greyhound racing. Softbound. $9.95. (ISBN: 0-89746-007-3)

**The Gambling Times Guide to Harness Racing** by Igor Kusyshyn, Ph.D., Al Stanley and Sam Dragich—Three of Canada's top harness handicapping authorities present their inside approach to analyzing the harness racing scene and selecting winners. All the important factors from the type of sulky, workouts, drivers' ratings, speed, pace, etc., are skillfully presented in simple terms that can be used by novices and experienced racegoers to find the likely winners. Softbound. $5.95. (ISBN: 0-89746-002-2)

**The Gambling Times Guide to Jai Alai** by William R. Keevers—The most comprehensive book on jai alai available. Author Bill Keevers takes the reader on an informative journey from the ancient beginnings of the game to its current popularity. This easy-to-understand guide will show you the fine points of the game, how to improve your betting percentage, and where to find jai alai frontons.
Softbound. $5.95. (ISBN: 0-89746-010-3)

**The Gambling Times Guide to Thoroughbred Racing** by R.G. Denis— Newcomers to the racetrack and veterans alike will appreciate the informative description of the thoroughbred pari-mutuel activity supplied by this experienced racing authority. Activities at the track and available information are blended skillfully in this guide to selecting winners that pay off in big-ticket returns.
Softbound. $5.95. (ISBN: 0-89746-005-7)

**Fast Track to Thoroughbred Profits** by Mark Cramer—Here is a unique and effective approach to selecting thoroughbred winners. *WIN* Magazine's horse racing editor and noted handicapping expert Cramer discusses how to distinguish between valuable and commonplace information through a method using handicapping factors in terms of ''return on investment.'' Experienced racing enthusiasts will find many surprises and ''edges'' in this work, while beginners will appreciate Cramer's clear and lively presentation.
Softbound. $8.95. (ISBN: 0-89746-025-1)

## Other Winning Programs From Gambling Times Software

Turn your computer into a home casino!!

**COMPLETE CRAPS**—Try your dice system without risk at home before you bet your cash in the casino! The experts at Gambling Times Software have devised the most complete craps program available today which includes every conceivable bet and playing system known. Realistic graphics and sound simulate actual casino play. This research and learning tool enables you to select the rules variations of your favorite casino. Select any system you like; a different system for every bet on the table...if you choose! Change your bets with each roll of the dice. Let "Complete Craps" play thousands of rolls, then see the results tallied and charted on the screen or printed out. Complete documentation included. (Minimum 256K and a floppy drive required; hard disk recommended. IBM-PC compatible only.) *Add $3 shipping and handling. $5 extra for 3½" version. Only $49.95!

**LOTTO CALC**—The ultimate lottery players' software! Harness the power of your IBM PC or PC-compatible to capture the data you need to knowledgeably play and BEAT any lotto game in the U.S., Canada or overseas. Three years in the making, this powerful database gives the serious lottery player: hit-and-miss frequencies, complete up-to-date records of every lotto game played in the U.S. from its inception, updating capability, accurate repeat occurrences, file merging plus WHEELING, random number selections and computer system picks. Complete documentation included. (Minimum 256K and a floppy drive required; hard disk recommended. IBM-PC compatible only.) *Add $3 shipping and handling. $5 extra for 3½" version. Only $49.95!

**EXPERT BLACKJACK**—WARNING: THIS IS NO GAME! "Expert Blackjack" is simply the most powerful analytical and learning tool available. Learn from modern masters of "21." Ken Uston, Julian Braun and Stanley Roberts have contributed their knowledge of blackjack and incorporated it into this learning and playing program designed for experts and beginners alike. Contains exclusive systems, teaches play, advises and charts your results. Don't go into the casino ill equipped to *WIN*. Simulate casino conditions with this program *before* heading for the tables and amaze yourself with the new-found strength of your game. $495

**COMPLETE BACCARAT**—The ultimate game for high rollers. Learn and practice the game, applying pre-programmed systems or design your own. For all varieties of the game from *punto banco* to *chemin-de-fer*. Single table or *deux tableaux*. Complete statistics charted on screen or printout. Complete documentation included. (Minimum 256K and a floppy drive required; hard disk recommended. IBM-PC compatible only.) *Add $3 shipping and handling. $5 extra for 3½" version. Only $49.95!

**COMPLETE ROULETTE**—French (0) or American (00) versions complete with the most popular pre-programmed systems, or design and implement your own favorite system. Allows you to run your system prior to laying down cash at a casino. Complete statistics charted on screen or printout. Complete documentation included. (Minimum 256K and a floppy drive required; hard disk recommended. IBM-PC compatible only.) *Add $3 shipping and handling. $5 extra for 3½" version. Only $49.95!

**SUPER 7-STUD POKER**—This all-new program allows you to program your opponents' playing and betting tendencies. Good for beginners and experts alike. Realistic graphics and sound let you feel like you're sitting in a real game! Results charted on screen or printout. Complete documentation included. (Minimum 256K and a floppy drive required; hard disk recommended. IBM-PC compatible only.) *Add $3 shipping and handling. $5 extra for 3½" version. Only $49.95!

## Ordering Information

Send your book or software order along with your check or money order to:

Gambling Times
16760 Stagg St., Suite 213
Van Nuys, CA 91406

*Softbound Books:* Please add $1.00 per bood if delivered in the United States, $1.50 in Canada or Mexico, and $3.50 for foreign countries.
*Hardbound Books:*Shipping charges for the following books are $2.50 if delivered in the United States, $3.00 in Canada or Mexico, and $5.00 for foreign countries:
*Caro's Book of Tells*
*Million Dollar Blackjack*
*P$yching Out Vegas*
*Winning Blackjack (softcover, large format)*
*Gambling and the Law*

# GLOSSARY

**ACE ADJUSTMENT**—Adjustment made to the running count for the purpose of determining size of bet.

**ACE-POOR**—When there is a lower than average number of aces remaining to be played. This condition favors the house.

**ACE-RICH**—When there is a higher than average number of aces remaining to be played. This condition favors the player.

**ACTION**—The total amount of money bet by the player(s) on all hands played; for example, one hundred and fifty bets of $5.00 each is $750.00 of action.

**BACK-COUNTING**—Counting down a deck or shoe, but not playing at the table. Usually the person back-counting is standing in back of the players at the table.

**BANK**—The playing stake of a player or a team.

**BAR**—To prohibit a player from playing (or sometimes even being in) a casino. To prevent the player from playing a table game — almost always Blackjack.

**BASIC STRATEGY**—The optimum way for a Blackjack player to play his/her hands without counting, using a prescribed set of house rules.

**BIG PLAYER**—The member of the team who bets the money (or the one who makes the BIG bets). Usually supported by the other team members who may bet only small amounts, or who may not bet at all.

**BETTING RATIO**—The mathematical ratio between the highest and the lowest bets placed by a player.

**BETTING TRUE COUNT**—The value of the true count, adjusted to reflect the number of aces rich or poor.

**BLACK**—The color of the $100.00 chip.

**BLACKJACK**—An ace and a ten-value card dealt to the player on the first two cards; this combination is also called a "natural" or a "snapper."

**BREAK IT DOWN**—To place chips into countable piles, or to separate them into colors.

**BREAK THE BANK**—To distribute to team members, the net amount won at Blackjack. In other words, to break up the bank and divide the money among the team members.

**BREAKING HAND**—A hand that will BREAK (go over 21) with a one-card draw, such as a hard 12, 13, 14, 15 or 16. Also called a "stiff."

**BURN**—The dealer's act of removing the first (or more) cards after the shuffle and placing the card(s) in the discard pile or at the bottom of the deck.

**BUST**—To exceed a playing total of "21."

**CAGE**—The location of the casino cashier.

**CHECK**—Gambling chip.

**COLD DECK**—A deck or decks unfavorable to the player — one that has a high minus count.

**COMP**—The privilege of using casino/hotel services free of charge usually given to a player who is designated as a high-roller.

**CONVERSION FACTOR (CF)**—The number by which the running count is divided (sometimes multiplied) to arrive at the true count. It is generally equal either to the number of full decks or half-decks that have NOT been put into play.

**COUNT**—Usually used to refer to the running count, which is the cumulative value of all cards played at any given time based on a set of preassigned values for each card denomination.

**COUNTER**—A player who uses a counting system to keep track of the cards played in order to determine whether the deck is favorable or unfavorable to the player.

**COVER**—Measures used by counters to disguise the fact that they are counters from casino personnel.

**COVER BET**—A bet made by the counter for the pit boss's benefit to disguise the fact that he is a counter. For example, the player/counter may make a large bet off the top of the deck, a small bet when the count is favorable, or a large bet when the count is unfavorable.

**COVER PLAY**—A play of the hand (usually a strategy error) made by a counter to disguise from the pit boss the fact that he is counting.

**CUTCARD**—A card, usually a solid colored piece of plastic, which is inserted into the cards in a deck or shoe to determine when the pack will be shuffled.

**DEALER**—An employee of the casino who deals the cards, makes the payoffs, sees that the rules are followed at his/her table and plays the deck(s) in accordance with a fixed specified set of instructions.

**DOUBLE DECK**—A Blackjack game played with two decks of cards.

**DOUBLE-DOWN**—An option that allows the player to double the value of his bet after looking at his (usually) first two cards. The player is dealt one additional card.

**DOUBLE EXPOSURE**—A Blackjack game in which both of the dealer's cards are shown to the player before the player plays his hand. In most such games, other rules are changed to restore to the house the overall edge.

**DOUBLE THE BANK**—The goal of most card counters or teams: to double the original playing stake or bank.

**DRAW**—To obtain additional cards to the original two cards dealt.

**DROP**—The total amount of cash plus the value of markers drawn at a table game (or for a shift, or an entire casino).

**DUMPING OFF**—The act by a cheating dealer of giving house money to a player usually a confederate or agent by overpaying bets and other techniques.

**EARLY SURRENDER**—A player's option of giving up half of the bet before the dealer checks to determine whether he/she has a Blackjack.

**ELEMENT-OF-RUIN**—The percentage likelihood that the player(s) will lose his/her (their) bank.

**EXPECTED VALUE**—The dollar amount that the player(s) should win (or lose) if encountering "average luck," that is, in exact accordance with the statistical advantage to the house.

**FACE CARD**—King, queen, jack.

**FILL**—The act of bringing additional checks (chips) to the table to replenish the dealer's rack.

**FIRST BASE**—The far right-hand seat at the Blackjack table. (The first player to receive cards.)

**FLASH**—To show a card, usually a dealer's hole card.

**FLAT BET**—To bet the same amount of money on each hand played. Usually done for cover purposes or in a hole card game.

**FLOORMAN**—The lowest echelon of pit personnel supervising a casino table game.

**FOREIGN CHECKS**—Checks from another casino.

**FRONT-LOADER**—A careless dealer who exposes the hole card in the process of dealing.

**FRONT-LOADING**—Observing the value of the dealer's hole card as it is inadvertently exposed during the process of dealing by a careless dealer.

**GREEN**—$25.00 chips usually green in color.

**HARD HAND**—A hand without an ace, or one with an ace that can only be counted one way; for example, an ace,6 and 9. The ace in this sequence can only be counted as one.

**HEAD-ON**—Playing alone against the dealer.

**HEAT**—Actions or statements by casino personnel that lead the player to believe he is suspected of being a counter.

**HIT**—To request another card from the dealer.

**HOLD**—The ratio between the win (amount won by the house) and the drop.

**HOLE CARD**—The dealer's bottom card, usually dealt face down and not exposed until after the players have played their hands.

**HOLE CARD PLAY**—A Blackjack play often involving more than one person. This play is based on the player's knowledge of the dealer's hole card; such as, but not limited to, front-loading and spooking.

**HOT DECK**—A deck or shoe favorable to the player.

**HUSTLING**—Hinting or asking a player for a tip or gift.

**INSURANCE**—A bet allowed when the dealer shows an ace. The player is allowed to bet half his original bet that the dealer has a 10 as his hole card, and thus a Blackjack. If the dealer does have a Blackjack, the Insurance bet is paid at two to one. The player loses his original bet unless he has a Blackjack in which case his original bet is pushed. If If the dealer does not have a Blackjack, the Insurance bet is lost and the play continues.

**INSURANCE COUNTER**—A player who uses a special count, perfect for the Insurance bet. He often signals the correct Insurance play to another counter who is playing a different system.

**JOINT BANK**—An arrangement where two or more players combine resources and play jointly off the total amount, sharing in the win or loss.

**LOADER**—A front-loader; a careless dealer who exposes the hole card in the process of dealing.

**MARKER**—A special casino check or draft used by the gambler to draw chips against his credit or money on deposit in the casino cage.

**MECHANIC**—A cheating dealer; generally one who deals seconds.

**MINUS COUNT**—A cumulative negative count of the cards placed in play; tends to be to the disadvantage of the player.

**MONEY MANAGEMENT**—The manipulation of increments of one's bankroll in betting, the better to overcome adverse house percentages.

**MULTIPLE DECK**—A Blackjack game played with two or more decks of cards; usually four or six decks.

**NATURAL**—See "Blackjack."

**NEGATIVE SWING**—A period, usually an extended one, during which the player shows a loss.

**NICKELS**—$5.00 chips.

**OFF-THE-TOP**—At the beginning of a deck or shoe, immediately after the shuffle.

**ON-THE-RAIL**—Observing a gambling game, but not playing it; in Blackjack, usually from behind the players (in poker, usually behind a rail that separates the players from the spectators).

**ON-THE-SQUARE**—On the up-and-up; fair.

**OUTSIDE MAN**—A casino employee who surreptitiously observes from outside the pit, usually pretending to be a patron. To casino employees: a non-casino employee, usually a cheat.

**PAIR SPLITTING**—See "Split."

**PAT HAND**—A hand totaling 17 through 21.

**PEEK**—The process of looking at a card. Normally, the dealer is said to peek when looking for a possible natural with an ace or 10 up-card. A cheating dealer will try to peek to determine the value of the top card of the undealt deck.

**PIT BOSS**—A casino official who supervises play at a group of gaming tables; often supervises the activities of several floormen.

**PLAYER'S ADVANTAGE**—The percent of money wagered that a player can expect to win in the long run: This number is computed by statistical methods and depends on the particular system the player employs. If a player enjoys a 2% advantage, he will win in the long run 2% of the total amount of money bet. If a player has a 0% expectation, he will break even over a period of time. If his expectation is -10%, he will eventually lose ten cents out of each dollar bet.

**POINT COUNT**—The evaluation of odds via a tally of assigned points. A number is assigned to each card according to the value of that card toward making up a winning hand for the player. For example, each 2,3,4,5 or 6 counts as +1; each 7,8 or 9 counts as 0; each 10,J,Q,K or ace counts as -1. The point count is computed at the end of each hand by adding the counts for each card played in that hand to the point count at the end of the previous hand.

**POOR**—The deck (or decks) is said to be poor in certain values of cards if there is a smaller-than-normal percentage of that card value present.

**PREFERENTIAL SHUFFLING**—The action by a dealer of shuffling up decks positive to the player and dealing out decks negative to the player.

**PRESS**—To increase the size of the subsequent wager.

**PULL UP A PLAY**—To call off a play in the casino — usually a counting or hole card play. This is usually accomplished by one player furtively signaling another.

**PUSH**—A tie or stand-off in which the player neither wins nor loses.

**QUARTERS**—$25.00 chips.

**RANK**—The defined value of each card. The nine of clubs has a rank of 9. The queen of spades has a rank of 10.

**RANK COUNT**—The number of a particular rank that has been played and counted. Refers to those systems where a particular rank, such as tens, aces or fives, is counted.

**RED**—$5.00 chips.

**RELAY**—A person who relays signals from one person to another in a casino.

**RICH**—The deck (or decks) is said to be rich in certain values of cards if there is a larger-than-normal percentage of cards present.

**RUNNING COUNT**—The cumulative value of all cards played at any given time based on a set of preassigned values for each card denomination.

**SECONDS**—Not dealing the top card from the deck; a form of cheating.

**SHILL**—A casino employee who plays to generate business for a casino game.

**SHOE**—A container used to hold undealt cards, usually used when four or more decks are used.

**SHORT SHOE**—A pack of cards dealt from a shoe which is not composed of complete decks; usually tens have been taken out (or fours or fives added) to the benefit of the cheating house.

**SILVER**—Silver dollars or $1.00 gaming tokens.

**SINGLE DECK**—A Blackjack game played with one deck almost always hand-held by the dealer.

**SIX DECK**—A Blackjack game played with six decks dealt from a shoe.

**SKY**—An area above the main casino where play is observed through one-way mirrors. Also, the employee(s) assigned to work in such an area; also called "eye-in-the-sky."

**SNAPPER**—See "Blackjack."

**SOFT HAND**—A hand with an ace which can be valued as "11."

**SPLIT**—An option allowing the player to make two cards of identical value into two hands betting an amount equal to the original wager on the second card. See "Pair Splitting."

**SPOOK**—A person who reads the hole card in a spooking play.

**SPOOKING**—Spotting the dealer's hole card from the rear, when the dealer checks to see if he has a Blackjack, and signaling that information to a player at the dealer's table.

**SPREAD**—To bet more than one hand, as "to spread to three hands of $500."

**STACKED DECK**—A pre-arranged sequence of cards used to cheat players.

**STAND**—A player's decision not to draw additional cards.

**STEAMING**—Betting higher and higher — usually after a series of losing hands. The out-of-control steamer is the pit boss's delight.

**STIFF**—See "Breaking Hand."

**STRIKE NUMBER**—The plus or minus count in a counting system at which the size of the bet or the play of the hand is varied.

**SURRENDER**—A decision made by a player to throw in his first two cards and Surrender half his bet. In Nevada this decision is made after it is ascertained that the dealer does not have Blackjack. If the player can surrender before the dealer turns his hole card, it is called *Early Surrender.* Surrender is not permitted in most casinos.

**TAKE IT OFF FROM THE INSIDE**—The act of stealing from the house by casino personnel.

**TAKE-OFF MAN**—The player, usually in a spooking or cheating operation, who bets the big money.

**TAP OUT**—To lose one's total bank.

**THIRD BASE**—The far left-hand seat at the Blackjack table. The last player before the dealer.

**TOKE**—A tip to the dealer or to other casino employees.

**TRUE COUNT**—The running count adjusted for the number of cards or decks remaining to be played. Also called just "True."

**"21"**—Another name for the game of Blackjack. Also, the winning total in Blackjack.

**UP CARD**—The dealer's card which is exposed to the player.

**WINDOW**—The space, usually between the left side of the (right-handed) dealer's body and his left upperarm, through which the value of his hole card is seen when he checks to see if he has a Blackjack. A spooking term.

**WIRED**—To have a good hand — usually a 20.

**ZONES**—A portion of a multiple-deck shoe which may be treated as if it were the beginning of a freshly shuffled deck.

# BIBLIOGRAPHY

Baldwin, Roger R.; Cantey, Wilbert E.; Maisel, Herbert; and McDermott, James P. "The Optimum Strategy in Blackjack." *Journal of the American Statistical Association,* September, 1956.

Braun, Julian H. *Development and Analysis of Winning Strategies for the Casino Game of Blackjack.* Las Vegas: Gambler's Book Club, 1974.

Braun, Julian H. *How to Play Winning Blackjack.* Chicago: Data House Publishing Co., Inc., 1980.

Canfield, Robert Albert. *Blackjack Your Way to Riche$.* Secaucus, N.J.: Lyle Stuart, Inc., 1979.

Collver, Donald L. *Scientific Blackjack & Complete Casino Guide.* New York: ARCO Publishing Company, 1971.

Epstein, Richard A. *The Theory of Gambling and Statistical Logic.* New York: Academic Press, 1967.

Einstein, Charles. *How to Win at Blackjack.* New York: Cornerstone Library, 1971.

Fristedt, Bert and Heath, David. "The Most Powerful Blackjack Strategy Ever Devised." *Winning,* May 1977.

Griffin, Peter A. "Use of Bivariate Normal Approximations to Evaluate Single Parameter Card Counting Systems in Blackjack." Paper presented to the Second Conference on Gambling. Lake Tahoe, June 1975.

Gwynn, John M., Jr., and Seri, Armand. "Experimental Comparisons of Blackjack Betting Systems." Paper presented to Fourth Conference on Gambling. Reno: December 1978.

Humble, Lance, Ph.D. *Blackjack Gold.* Thornhill, Ontario, Canada: International Gaming Incorporated, 1976.

Humble, Lance, Ph.D. *Blackjack Super Gold.* Las Vegas: B & G Publishing Co., Inc., 1979.

Humble, Lance, Ph.D. *HI-OPT I: Multiparameter Tables.* Thornhill, Ontario, Canada: International Gaming, 1977.

Humble, Lance, Ph.D. and Cooper, Carl, Ph.D. *The World's Greatest Blackjack Book.* New York: Doubleday & Co., 1980.

Miller, Len. *The Gambling Times Guide to Casino Games.* Hollywood: Gambling Times, Inc., 1983.

Mitchell, D. Howard. "Blackjack Systems from Basic Strategy to Expert." *Gambling Times,* February 1978.

Mitchell, D. Howard. *The DHM System: A Winning Strategy for Four Deck Blackjack.* San Dimas, CA: DHM Associates, 1974.

Nolan, Walter I. *The Facts of Blackjack.* Las Vegas: Gambler's Book Club, 1976.

Patterson, Jerry L. *Blackjack: A Winner's Handbook.* Voorhees, N.J.: Echelon Enterprises, 1977.

Patterson, Jerry L. *Blackjack's Winning Formula.* New York: Perigee Books, G.P. Putnam's Sons, 1982.

Patterson, Jerry L. and Jay, Walter. *Casino Gambling: Winning Techniques for Craps, Roulette, Blackjack and Baccarat.* New York: Perigee Books, G.P. Putnam's Sons, 1982.

Revere, Lawrence. *Playing Blackjack as a Business.* Las Vegas: Paul Mann Publishing Co. 1973.

Roberts, Stanley. *The Beginner's Guide to Winning Blackjack.* Hollywood, CA: Gambling Times Incorporated, 1984.

Roberts, Stanley. *How to Win at Weekend Blackjack.* Los Angeles: Scientific Research Services, 1973.

Roberts, Stanley. *Winning Blackjack.* Los Angeles: Scientific Research Services, 1971.

Sklansky, David. "Getting the Best of It: The Key Card Concept—An Extra Edge at the Blackjack Table." *Gambling Times,* August 1977.

Skolnick, Jerome. *House of Cards.* Boston: Little, Brown, 1978.

Smith, Harold, Jr. *I Want to Quit Winners.* Englewood Cliffs, N.J.: Prentice-Hall, 1961.

Snyder, Arnold. *The Blackjack Formula.* Berkeley, CA: RGE, 1980.

Snyder, Arnold. *Blackjack for Profit.* Berkeley, CA: RGE, 1981.

Snyder, Arnold. *Blackbelt in Blackjack.* Berkeley, CA: RGE, 1983.

Snyder, Arnold. *Blackjack Forum,* (Journal). Berkeley, CA: RGE, 1981.

Thorp, Edward O., Ph. D. *Beat the Dealer.* New York: Random House, 1962.

Thorp, Edward O., Ph. D. *Beat the Dealer,* 2nd Edition. New York: Vintage Books, 1966.

Thorp, Edward O., Ph.D. "Fortune's Formula: The Game of Blackjack." *Notices of the American Mathematical Society,* December 1960.

Thorp, Edward O. "Probabilities and Strategies for the Game of Faro: Appendix. Possible Application of Nonrandom Shuffling to Blackjack." *Gambling and Society,* edited by William R. Eadington. Springfield, IL: Charles C. Thomas, 1976.

Thorp, Edward O., Ph.D. *The Mathematics of Gambling.* Hollywood, CA: Gambling Times Incorporated, 1984.

Uston, Kenneth, and Rapaport, R. *The Big Player.* New York: Holt, Rinehart, and Winston, 1977.

Uston, Kenneth. *Million Dollar Blackjack.* Hollywood, CA: Gambling Times, Inc., 1981.

Uston, Kenneth. *One-Third of a Shoe.* Wheaton, MD: Uston Institute of Blackjack, 1979.

Wilson, Allan N. *The Casino Gambler's Guide.* New York: Harper & Row, 1965.

# INDEX

# Index

# Gambling Books Ordering Information

**Ask for any of the books listed below at your bookstore.** Or to order direct from the publisher, call 1-800-447-BOOK (MasterCard or Visa), or send a check or money order for the books purchased (plus $3.00 shipping and handling for the first book ordered and 50¢ for each additional book) to Carol Publishing Group, 120 Enterprise Avenue, Dept. 6015, Secaucus, NJ 07094.

**Beating the Wheel: The System That's Won More Than $6 Million, From Las Vegas to Monte Carlo** by Russell T. Barnhart
A unique system that can be learned quickly and easily for profiting from roulette, based on escalating small bets.
$12.95 paper 0-8184-0553-8 (CAN $15.95)

**Blackjack Your Way to Riches** by Richard Albert Canfield
A highly prized secret system that shows how it is possible to win at any rate you choose. Information on money management and the right method of preserving and building capital.
$9.95 paper 0-8184-0498-1 (CAN $12.95)

**Darwin Ortiz on Casino Gambling: The Complete Guide to Playing and Winning**
Since what gamblers don't know *can* hurt them, this book answers all your questions, regardless of their wagering level.
$12.95 paper 0-8184-0525-2 (CAN $16.95)

**Gambling Times Guide to Blackjack** by Stanley Roberts
Learn the secrets of such blackjack pros as Julian Braun, Lance Humble, and Jerry Patterson, no matter what your wagering level.
$9.95 paper 0-89746-015-4 (CAN $12.95)

**Gambling Times Guide to Craps** by N.B. Winkless, Jr.
Introduces you to the buy table, the superficial complexities, the best bets, the layout, the language, the math, and the systems of craps.
$9.95 paper 0-89746-013-8 (CAN $12.95)

**How to be Treated Like a High Roller** by Robert Renneisen
The President of the Claridge in Atlantic City reveals how to take advantage of casino "comps."
$7.95 paper 0-8184-0556-2 (CAN $9.95)

**John Patrick's Craps**
A professional gambler, and host of a national television show, as well as dozens of instructional videotapes about gambling, John Patrick shares his secrets of success, providing specific, easy-to-learn methods for mastering the tables.
$14.95 paper 0-8184-0554-6 (CAN $18.95)
**Also available: John Patrick's Blackjack**
$12.95 paper 0-8184-0555-4 (CAN $16.95)

**Million Dollar Blackjack** by Ken Uston
A method that can turn any average player into a top-notch professional. "One of the best blackjack players in the world, and the most controversial."—*The New York Times*
$16.95 paper 0-89746-068-5 (CAN $21.95)

**Playing Blackjack as a Business** by Lawrence Revere
This easy-to-understand book features strategies devised from computer runs by Julian H. Bruan of IBM, recognized as the most capable man in the world in this field.
$14.95 paper 0-8184-0064-1 (CAN $18.95)

**Progression Blackjack: Exposing the Cardcounting Myth** by Donald Dahl
A proven winning strategy for novices and veterans alike which renders previous books obsolete.
$8.95 paper 0-8065-1396-9 (CAN $10.95)

**Psyching Out Vegas** by Marvin Karlins, Ph.D.
Shows how casino operators try to psych gamblers into losing—and reveals how to turn dealers into much-needed friends.
$15.00 cloth 0-914314-03-3 (CAN $19.95)

**Winning at Slot Machines** by Jim Regan
Increase your chances of winning money by learning what makes slots actually pay off. Included is information on gaming laws and the rules of gaming conduct.
$5.95 paper 0-8065-0973-2 (CAN $7.95)

**Winning Blackjack in Atlantic City and Around the World** by Thomas Gaffney
Pointers on winning blackjack in any of the world's casinos, but aimed primarily at the Atlantic City game: one in which they play with a six deck shuffle.
$7.95 paper 0-8065-1178-8 (CAN $10.95)

**Winning Blackjack Without Counting Cards** by David S. Popik
Outlines a basic strategy which players can use to gain a percentage of the house with no cardcounting.
$7.95 paper 0-8065-0963-5 (CAN $10.95)

(Prices subject to change; books subject to availability)